Netflix and streaming ~~~~

With gratitude to those who've been patient and generous.

Netflix and Streaming Video

The Business of Subscriber-Funded Video on Demand

Amanda D. Lotz

polity

First published in 2022 by Polity Press

Polity Press
65 Bridge Street
Cambridge CB2 1UR, UK

Polity Press
101 Station Landing
Suite 300
Medford, MA 02155, USA

ISBN-13: 978-1-5095-5294-8
ISBN-13: 978-1-5095-5295-5 (pb)

A catalogue record for this book is available from the British Library.

Library of Congress Control Number: 2021946445

Typeset in 11 on 13pt Sabon
by Fakenham Prepress Solutions, Fakenham, Norfolk NR21 8NL
Printed and bound in Great Britain by TJ Books Ltd, Padstow, Cornwall

The publisher has used its best endeavours to ensure that the URLs for external websites referred to in this book are correct and active at the time of going to press. However, the publisher has no responsibility for the websites and can make no guarantee that a site will remain live or that the content is or will remain appropriate.

Every effort has been made to trace all copyright holders, but if any have been overlooked the publisher will be pleased to include any necessary credits in any subsequent reprint or edition.

For further information on Polity, visit our website:
politybooks.com

Contents

Contents

Figures and Tables

All figures and tables created by the author based on data from Ampere Analysis.

Preface

I didn't mean to write this book. From mid-2019, my weekly intended 'to do' list included a steadily ignored item of 'pull together thinking about SVODs' (subscriber-funded video on-demand services). I ignored it because I couldn't find a point or argument to organize that thinking. I had promised Mary Savigar at Polity to consider a book about 'streaming' a couple of years earlier and had made similar progress. My writing process remained constipated, unable to sort lots of little arguments into anything big enough to warrant a book or, frankly, compelling enough for an article.

But with the lockdown in March 2020, my deck cleared. I wasn't teaching, my kids were old enough to manage with minimal intervention the brief period of home school Australia endured, and I needed something to occupy my anxiety. I started with a list of the little arguments or things that I felt were misunderstood which I had been stewing over since it became clear Netflix would not quickly flame out, like so many other internet-distributed video enterprises I'd monitored over

Preface

the last two decades. I converted the arguments into questions and began 'answering' each in a blog post.

These were written quickly because I had been thinking about them since I turned my attention to streaming services around 2015. The earliest version of that thinking appears in *Portals: A Treatise on Internet-Distributed Television* (2017), which was most notable at that time for arguing that subscriber-funded services such as Netflix were quite different from YouTube, and that this difference in business model required as much reconsideration of our theories and assumptions as the use of the internet as a distribution technology. That seems quite obvious now, but, of course, a lot has changed in just a few years.

The blogs were a freeing form of writing. I was not sure for whom I was writing and, for once, didn't care. It would be fair to categorize them as a response to the accumulation of all the wrong takes I'd seen in my Twitter feed and popular journalism, but also as frustration with scholarship that framed the services too strongly in terms of past technologies. I wrote back to the financial analysts who carried on about comparing what Netflix paid for *The Irishman* with estimates of its viewing, to critics who attributed critique of an entire service to their experience of a few shows, and to those among my scholarly community – though mostly not those actually writing and researching centrally in the area – who seemed to be approaching these services without really appreciating their industrial differences. The task of formulating coherent arguments in response to things commonly misperceived because of uninterrogated assumptions – for example, that these services were 'like' linear channels – helped me work through a lot of clutter that

ix

had been half-formed conceptualization in the corners of my brain.

Once there were thirty blog posts and nearly 50,000 words, I wondered if there was indeed a book here. I set it aside for a few months, and Mary generously sought a couple of reviews. The problem remained the same, though: what was the point? A book with a bunch of middle-level arguments didn't seem particularly purposeful, and who was I writing for anyhow? When I returned with fresh eyes, I could see two arguments into which most of the smaller 'questions' actually fit. I restructured to build those arguments, cast off those posts that didn't fit, and wrote new introductory material and bits throughout. We identified the audience as people interested in understanding the characteristics of these services who are the readers of the regular stream of journalism about them – this is not a theoretical deep dive, and I planed the edges where my annoyance was too raw (it was lockdown times; we were all just trying not to lose our minds).

Those arguments structure the book's two main sections: 1) that subscriber-funded video streaming services require distinct conceptualization from video services that have used other distribution technologies and business models, and 2) that Netflix is doing something different from past services *and* other subscriber-funded video streamers. I see my intervention here as setting the table for building understanding, research, and policy about the particular economic and technological characteristics of this sector of streaming service – a foundation rather than the embodiment of the work that remains needed. My articles offer more proper scholarship for those that seek specific inquiries, evidence, and engagement with literature. Citation here is light, in line with the intended audience, and often used to avoid extensive discussion of something I've written about elsewhere. The blog origins mean the book is not rigidly linear. Chapters lack the formality of conventional introductions and conclusions to keep the discussion moving and are largely discrete meditations that can be read in any order.

These pages provide an accumulation of more than five years of thinking that is built from testing the continued relevance of as much 'common sense' as I could see in pursuit of conceptualizing SVODs relative to what has come before, as well as their distinct affordances. It is thinking built from a lot of 'what if?' and 'why?' questions, and it is deeply researched even if writing with an academic-light focus has led to sparse citations. Notably, unlike my other research, it relies little on interviews – no, Netflix won't answer my requests either. But I have watched, read, and listened to every public utterance I could find.

What I'm offering or arguing for here is a paradigm of thinking. It eschews a lot of the conventional wisdom. To be clear, this book focuses on SVODs because they are a new thing with distinctive features that need to be explained, and not because they are now the most important part of audiovisual ecosystems. These services remain responsible for a minority of time spent with video even in countries in which they have been widely adopted. While they may become a dominant form of scripted fiction delivery for those who can afford them, I don't expect linear services or cinemagoing to disappear in my lifetime. I don't think we yet know if they are profoundly important or how they matter to the major culture and society questions that are central to the field, but they are on pace to be something that media and cultural studies scholars need to understand. I offer a systematically built conceptual frame from which to ask specific questions about SVODs that are increasingly important to cultural producers and circulators, questions that this particular book doesn't have the scope to answer.

This is perhaps, to a degree, *Portals 2: A Manifesto on Internet-Distributed Video*, but maybe not as much of a polemic as 'manifesto' might suggest. At this point, what I've written here has come to seem quite obvious and basic, yet I know that it has taken the better part of five years to sort out and present coherently. At the least, it explains why I've taken some contrarian positions in my articles about streaming and have come to see evidence of revolution over evolution, but it is offered mainly in the hope that others can use it as a foundation to spring into the interesting and important questions these services provoke.

Although only my name appears as author, Ramon Lobato has been a crucial interlocutor, and Dan Herbert, Lee Marshall, Aswin Punathambekar and several students and colleagues at the University of Michigan and Queensland University of Technology engaged in conversations helpful in testing these ideas. In 2016, Ramon and I co-created the Global Internet Television Consortium because it was so difficult to understand the role and impact of transnational SVODs outside of where we lived (I am an American who has lived in Australia since 2019). The detailed dossiers written by colleagues all over the world and available on the consortium website (https://global-internet-tv. com/) inform my understanding of SVODs globally, as does collaborative research with Ramon, Stuart Cunningham, and Alexa Scarlata derived from research funded from 2019 to 2021 by the Australian Research Council Discovery Programme (DP190100978).

Acknowledgements

The thinking here was instigated by many people, more than I can name, and several of whom I do not personally know. Earlier thoughts were shaped in conversations about streaming with Lee Marshall, Dan Herbert, and David Hesmondhalgh and in podcasts with Alex Intner. My depth of appreciation for the various forms that subscriber-funded video on-demand services (SVODs) take outside the US is particularly indebted to Ramon Lobato and our collaborative coordination of the Global Internet-Distributed Television Consortium (https://global-internet-tv.com/). I don't think either of us knew what we were endeavouring upon in 2016, just that our geographic positions prevented us from seeing much of the emerging picture of transnational streamers and that we needed colleagues to talk with about it. The dossiers contributed by the network of scholars have provided fascinating insight and been particularly formative in my thinking about 'global' strategy and the roles of SVODs.

The opportunity of an Australian Research Council Discovery Project with Ramon, Stuart Cunningham, and Alexa Scarlata has also provided a venue for a lot of the

Acknowledgements

idea building collected here. Many long conversations with Ramon are captured in our 2021 *Media Industries* journal article, which led to a bit of conceptual stability from which much of the conclusions here derive, and I have appreciated having the audience of the DP team to talk out preliminary notions. Oliver Eklund has also provided exquisite research assistance and must be credited for wrangling the data figures in the following pages. Claire Darling also supported the initial blog version of the writing.

Many of the ideas here might be stronger had there been more opportunity to test them in conferences and chats over the last year, but the pandemic denied that opportunity. My thanks to Cathy Johnson, Jonathan Gray, Aswin Punathambekar, and Cynthia Myers for providing remote support and to Kevin Sanson and Anna Potter for both personal and professional community in my new Australian life. Many members of the Global International-Distributed Television Consortium have also been crucial interlocutors, not just through their writing and thinking but have generously fielded my emails and inquiries.

My thanks as well to Mary Savigar, Stephanie Homer, and the team at Polity for your patience and persistence regarding the idea for this book and for your willingness to embrace its not wholly conventional form. My gratitude to the reviewers as well for smart suggestions and supporting the vision for the book.

Most of these pages were written only because I was left alone with my mind while my partner Wes sorted all manner of sibling squabbling and screen-time management through lockdown, for which I'm very grateful. Calla and Sayre have become expert SVOD users and offer me new vantage points on streaming

Acknowledgements

services. They have also provided crucial community as we've tried to make our way in a new place while often bound to our house. My love and gratitude to them, always.

Introduction

I wanted to call this *The SVOD Book*, but that is a pretty a terrible title. Terrible, but precise. SVOD may be the least elegant of all the terms that I and others have used over the last two decades to talk about video delivered by internet communication technologies and watched mostly in the home. An acronym for *subscriber-funded video on demand*, SVOD emerged alongside OTT (over the top), streaming, internet television, web TV, and a handful of other terms that are generally meant to indicate internet-distributed video. The two characteristics that are most meaningful in differentiating the operation of the particular type of video streaming service that has substantially adjusted the landscape of home video is clearly distinguished only in SVOD and noted in those four letters: these services are subscriber funded and available on demand.

I wanted a terrible but precise title because the variety of ways we can now access television and film has made them very complicated to discuss. The differences in both distribution technology – broadcast, cable, satellite, or internet – and funding mechanism

– advertising, transaction, subscriber payment, or public funds – have led to much greater industrial diversity among video services than was once the case. This book examines only SVOD services because relying solely on subscriber funding and allowing consumers on-demand access enables them to deviate significantly from many of the norms upon which the television and film industries have long operated. The different *technological capabilities* of these services – capabilities enabled by internet distribution – and the content strategies possible because they offer *content on demand and seek payment from viewers* rather than advertisers make them profoundly unlike the video industries in place for the last seventy years, and this book explores those differences. SVOD is precise but is more technical than common in most conversations. SVODs have entered the fabric of everyday life for many millions of homes, yet the acronym remains one that few use. Most people think of these simply as video streaming services, which is a broader category than is examined here.

This book does not aim to explore the entirety of internet-distributed video, and thus there are significant forms that are not discussed here.[1] Internet-distributed video also includes video found on social media such as Facebook, YouTube, and TikTok, which, to date, have been supported predominantly by advertisements and sponsor/influencer messaging. Their reliance on feeds, timelines, and non-linear channels also provides on-demand access, though sometimes these services offer live feeds as well. Furthermore, they are strongly distinguished by their openness in allowing almost anyone to upload video. This enables them to offer non-industrial forms of video creation, though the creators that earn a living from social video are increasingly every bit as 'professional' as those creating for SVODs. The reliance on advertising and the logics of social media require bespoke theory building for these forms of streaming video.

Another part of the advertiser-funded, internet-distributed video sector encompasses the many services that began as 'catch-up' services that evolved from linear channels to offer access to shows viewers missed at a scheduled viewing time.[2] Many now license and offer additional programming that never airs in the broadcast schedule, and a whole other group of AVOD (ad-funded video on demand) and FAST (free, ad-supported streaming television that is linear) services have no analogue precursor (Crackle, Roku TV, Tubi, Vudu, PlutoTV). To add further complexity, some services (Hulu, Peacock, HBO Max) offer separate ad- and subscriber-funded tiers in some countries and differentiate their offer based on the inclusion of commercials and/or particular content by tier.

Yet another category significant outside the US are VOD services supported by public-service media, some of which have ads while others rely on public funds. Those reliant on ads warrant consideration with AVODs, at least in terms of industrial positioning. Public-service media are also distinct from the central focus here, which is on commercial video services or services whose foremost mandate is pursuit of profit. The book contrasts SVODs many times throughout its pages with 'linear ad-supported services'. Technically, these are commercial (not public service), linear ad-supported services.[3]

The purpose of this book is not to map these variations but to investigate in great depth the particular dynamics of commercial on-demand video services that are not driven primarily by concerns of selling attention to advertisers. The landscape of SVOD, AVOD/FAST, and publicly funded VOD varies a lot from country to country, although several services are notable for their transnational availability. Much of this book focuses on transnational SVODs because they are having the biggest effect on restructuring video ecosystems worldwide. That doesn't make them the most important in every country; in fact dominance at the national level isn't to be expected in countries with the capital and scale to offer their own services. But it is also impossible for a single book to address highly particularized national dynamics, which drives the examples here to the transnational cases.

In addition to the ways in which SVODs are distinguished by *on-demand access* and *subscriber funding*, *multinational reach* differentiates several of the largest services. The origins of television and film industries were largely national, although they have grown more transnational over the decades, especially once the technology of internet distribution expanded the significant internationalization introduced by satellite in the 1990s. Multinational reach takes advantage of economies of scale that operate for media industries because the goods they offer have low to no marginal cost. The world of SVODs is thus simultaneously nationally distinctive and transnationally influenced.

This project constructs a foundation for analysing SVODs by teasing apart their similarities and differences from the video services that have been the basis of existing knowledge. It focuses on SVODs offering scripted fiction – or what we've known as drama and comedy series and movies. If successful, the insights here will assist others in contextualized analysis of more specialized services and particular national contexts. The first section of this book explores the industrial differences between SVODs and norms and practices we've come to expect from experience with linear ad-supported television services and theatrical distribution and why those differences matter. In order to address both general features of SVODs and the particularity of Netflix, the second section focuses on Netflix and how it is unlike most other SVODs. Somehow, we have arrived at page 5 without using a key word for a book about SVODs published in 2022: Netflix. By many measures, Netflix was the dominant SVOD as I wrote in 2021, and by many other measures it was an unusual SVOD. This dynamic required the structure of the book, which is built around two related but distinct arguments. Part I explores how subscriber-funded video-streaming services are distinct from video services that have used other distribution technologies and business models and provide the foundation of our industrial frameworks. Part II uses the case of Netflix, a more mature and pure-play service that differs from both past services *and* other subscriber-funded video streamers in key ways.

Writing a book about SVODs is made tricky by their continued and steady evolution. I've been studying the changes in the business of television since the early 2000s, and the only thing more certain twenty years later is that the industry is never going back to the way things were. In a book published in 2007, I identified the beginning of this change by proclaiming a start of the 'post-network era'. I knew then that internet distribution of video would change these industries profoundly but could hardly imagine how this change would come to be or how long it would take.

Introduction

We've passed many milestones of change in viewer and industry behaviour that make that eventual new normal more imaginable, but we have not yet reached a new stasis. I write with considerable hesitation, knowing the evolution of this sector has been both steady and extensive. From the vantage point of 2022, the multinational expansion of multiple US-based SVODs affiliated with major media conglomerates appears a particularly significant disruption of a wide range of status quo practices, and so the book focuses on this sector. Other consequential adjustments will transpire, and, as a result, this may merely be a first edition of my imagined *SVOD Book*, or perhaps SVOD services will prove a phase in a longer transition that necessitates a different focus to explain whatever comes next. The book is not without limits – notably, Chinese internet-distributed video does not neatly divide its universe so clearly among ad- and subscriber-funded services and requires bespoke foundation building. There is also a strong English-language bias towards the services on which I focus, despite notable transnational expansion from Viu, ZEE5, and others.

In concentrating on the general economic and techno-logical foundation of SVODs, this book aims to be relevant to readers in all countries. But because even global SVODs are understood and experienced within a national context, it is impossible to make claims consistently accurate across nations. Instead, the analysis here attempts to illustrate how we might explore the particular national industrial, cultural, regulatory, and historical contexts that make these dynamics just a little bit different everywhere through drawing out cases placed in either the Australian or US contexts in which I have most expertise.

Introduction

Dissecting the SVOD sector

Subscriber funding and provision of video on demand may make for a common sector, but the SVOD sector is composed of a complex taxonomy of distinctions.[4] At least four different structuring characteristics distinguish SVODs in ways that lead them to different strategies: geographic reach, library specificity, library ownership, and corporate ownership. These characteristics do not reliably align; instead, imagine them as reels on a slot machine so that any mix of characteristics might come up in combination, although some combinations are more common than others. Each blend of characteristics leads to different norms, behaviours, and priorities.

Geographic reach is the first significant characteristic. Lobato offers three variations: national-single territory, transnational multi-territory, and transnational global,[5] but, for simplicity, let's use *single territory*, *multi-territory*, and *global*. Of course these offer more of a continuum than three discreet variations – technically multi-territory might encompass everything from two to nearly two hundred territories, and global doesn't necessarily mean everywhere but a strategy based on being in most places and particularly in major markets. For the consideration here, the multi-territory variation might distinguish services in a handful of territories that probably have some reason for this middling scope, such as serving a geographic region or uniting communities with particular linguistic or cultural commonalities. Geographic reach is important because of the scale that becomes available to a service outside a single territory and the extent to which that scale enables particular content strategies.

Figure 1   Variation in the structuring characteristics of SVODs

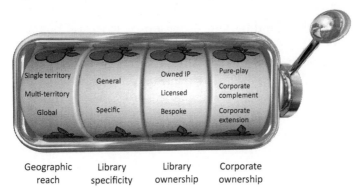

| Geographic reach | Library specificity | Library ownership | Corporate ownership |

The independent reels of the slot machine represent the various combinations of structuring characteristics among SVODs.

Library specificity might be best thought of as a dichotomy between *general* and *specific*, though here, too, services can be organized on a continuum. General libraries offer a range of content; they are the department store/Walmart/Target of the SVOD universe. A general library won't have everything or depth in many types of titles but provides a mix. In contrast, specific libraries are often based on a value proposition of providing uncommon depth of a single type of content. Specialty services won't be attractive to all consumers but are highly valuable to those that prefer the content on offer, a level of desire that may lead to willingness to pay more. They are like shoe stores in the retail comparison; they offer only one thing but provide much greater choice than the shoe options available in the department store. As with geographic reach, the degree of library specificity considerably structures much of the business and content strategy of an SVOD. It also indicates how the relationship among

SVODs is often more complementary than directly competitive. Just as both department stores and shoe stores can thrive, so too can general and specialty services coexist.

Library ownership identifies the distinction between services based on *owned IP* (intellectual property) or a library of owned titles, while other services rely on *licensed* libraries. A finer variation involves whether that owned IP is *bespoke*, or created particularly for the SVOD, or whether the titles were created over time for other television channels or movies for theatrical release. Distinguishing bespoke content developed specifically for the SVOD is important because services are able to deploy explicit content strategies through these titles. Bespoke content is a small amount of the content available on SVODs, and, to date, only Apple TV+ offers an entirely bespoke library. Many libraries are characterized by a blend of these attributes – for example, a mix of licensed and owned IP. Thus a key way of distinguishing SVODs by this characteristic is by the ratio of titles with these attributes. Table 1 lists some of the most subscribed services and captures data regarding their library size and number of commissioned titles to demonstrate the variation in the marketplace in 2021.[6]

As table 1 indicates, several services have commissioned titles for their SVOD, but such titles account for a negligible amount of the library in all but a very few services. This data is drawn from early 2021, which marks a preliminary moment for many of these services. A decade from now, the library categorizations of the predominantly owned-IP services will likely be more blended, but the table is helpful for indicating a distinction of Netflix as of 2021, especially from

Table 1 Different library and service characteristics

Service	Library size	Commissioned content (no.)	Commissioned content (%)	Geo reach	Specificity	Library ownership	Corporate position
Netflix	5,699	1,495	26%	Global	General	Licensed/bespoke	Pure play
Amazon Prime Video	19,067	196	1%	Global	General	Predominantly licensed	Corp complement
Hulu	2,718	111	4%	Single territory	General	Predominantly owned IP	Corp extension
Disney+	1,191	71	6%	Global	General	Predominantly owned IP	Corp extension
Paramount+	1,223	52	4%	Global	General	Predominantly owned IP	Corp extension
Apple TV+	52	41	79%	Global	General	Bespoke	Corp complement
Stan (AU)	2,896	23	1%	Single territory	General	Predominantly licensed	Corp extension
Acorn	353	0	0%	Multi-territory	Specific	Licensed	Corp extension
Crunchyroll	1,082	0	0%	Global	Specific	Licensed	Pure play>corp extension

This table contrasts key features of the libraries of several major SVODs.

the other global services that lack significant owned IP (Amazon Prime Video, Apple TV+). Including as counterpoints Stan, an Australian-only general entertainment service, Acorn, a multinational specialty drama service, and Crunchyroll, a global specialty service offering anime, illustrates how single-nation and speciality services can offer much smaller but distinctive libraries and still provide a value proposition that attracts enough subscribers to be regarded as successful.

Library ownership delimits content strategies in crucial ways that relate to the cost of content faced by the service and the extent to which it enables the service to offer a specific value proposition through bespoke content or simply through a valued experience. Although owning a significant library of titles is a considerable advantage, most services with substantial owned IP as of 2022 have built those libraries by making content for other commissioners or competitive dynamics. As a result, predominantly owned-IP SVODs tend to lack a clear or bespoke content strategy – at least at this early point in their development.

Finally, corporate position is a significant characteristic in distinguishing among SVODs. Corporate position references how the SVOD fits in a broader company strategy. Some SVODs – such as Netflix – are stand-alone businesses; most others are part of conglomerates and consequently may be valued for more than their contribution to revenue. The owned-IP SVODs are part of media conglomerates and thus offer a new means of distribution for companies with long histories in video production and distribution. Others, such as AppleTV+, Amazon Prime Video, and even Peacock hold quite complicated corporate positions. These SVODs do indeed provide video, but it is unclear whether their corporate owners evaluate them with anything like the measures Netflix uses to assess its performance. These SVODs are part of a suite of products that in some cases may function as loss leaders or part of a bundle of goods used strategically in support of another more important product.

We might consider this as a contrast among SVODs with *pure play, corporate extension,* and *corporate complement* variations. Pure plays are single-purpose companies (Netflix); corporate extensions are SVODs that introduce a new distribution business to an existing video business (Disney+, discovery+); and corporate complements use video for reasons distinct from entertainment (Apple TV+, Amazon Prime Video).[7] These variations matter because they can lead SVODs to behave very differently as a result of their purpose to the company and what the company's goal for them is. A pure play focuses on subscriber metrics, while corporate complements might be considered successful based entirely on other metrics (e.g., number of Amazon Prime memberships; Apple device owners that upgrade to new services or products). A significant amount of variation can be found just among corporate complements. These different metrics of success also explain various approaches and funding levels evident among different services.

In time, these particular distinguishing characteristics may grow less varied and other differentiating features more pronounced. For instance, there is no measure of in-country scale of adoption here because very few have come to be mass-market services (subscribed to by a majority of homes in a country). The difference among services that are niche (less than 10 per cent of homes), significant (10 to 50 per cent), or mass (greater than

50 per cent) in terms of national subscriber bases may
come to be a significant structuring characteristic.

Subscriber-funded streamers are easily confused as being like other video services

Most of this book addresses how SVODs differ from the
linear services that have dominated video distribution
to the home. Those services provide a natural vantage
point through which to understand SVODs; however,
the substantial industrial differences of SVODs – their
business model, on-demand delivery, and transnational reach – also differentiate them from those other
video services and require different conceptual framing.
Understanding SVODs in relation to past norms requires
appreciating how they embody *both* change from *and*
continuity with pre-existing forms of video distribution.

To a large degree, our sense that SVODs are like
television channels derives from how they seem to do
the same task of delivering video as 'television' has
done and continues to do. The invisibility of the infrastructure that makes it possible for images to appear on
our screen likely accounts for that conceptual blurriness.
Notably, we also used our televisions to watch the VHS
tapes and DVDs we bought or rented, but I don't think
we ever considered them 'television' in the way we
might do with SVODs. From the perspective of the
living room sofa, SVODs can indeed seem quite similar
to television, and some national regulatory regimes –
most notably the European Union – have taken this
position with considerable industrial consequence. But
to properly understand SVODs, it is critical to appreciate their differences from norms of linear – especially

ad-supported – services in their underlying business model and metrics.

As long the pattern when new technologies are introduced, we have attempted to make sense of SVODs through the lenses of previous video distribution technologies. Because the first SVODs relied on enticing subscribers with content created for other services – typically programmes for television channels or movies originally created for theatrical release – it was easy to view them as like other services that performed a similar role. In this context, the content offered by SVODs was very much consistent with that offered by many broadcast and cable/satellite channels. Despite their different distribution technology, SVODs initially adhered fairly well to television's practices of offering hours of scripted fiction programming and much of the licensed content was created for a channel in another time or place. But SVODs also exhibited features more similar to video rental in providing access to a selection of content that could be chosen for viewing at a time of your choice in exchange for payment. Still, the situation of SVODs differs because it is based on selling access to a library, not attracting viewing to particular titles.[8] All of these features affect what type of content the services are likely to create or license and lead them to value different metrics than ad-supported video. Chapter 4 makes this industrial comparison in more detail. Of these frames, the presumption of SVODs being 'like' television probably pervades because television has been central to video consumption in the home for so long.

As the ecosystem of video services and content – and our use of them – has evolved, distinctions, such as Lynn Spiegel's categorization of 'television' as distinguished or determined by a combination of technology, industrial formations, government policies, and viewing practices, have become more difficult to apply. The technologies, industrial formations, government policies, and viewing practices that increasingly support the video watched daily have become multifaceted, and different norms have developed dependent on characteristics such as business model and distribution technology.[9] The distinction between media and delivery systems that Henry Jenkins makes in the introduction of *Convergence Culture* (2006) has been the foundation of my under-standing of SVODs as a sector of *internet-distributed video*, not a separate *type of medium* – which was how internet-distributed video was initially perceived (e.g. new media; internet video; web series).

Despite their similarities to pre-existing technologies of television and movie circulation, some SVODs have created a conceptual disjuncture by refusing to be merely another window for content created for television and theatrical distribution – although they also do this. The content SVODs have commissioned and those titles that are exclusive to their services (typically within a country) have created significant dilemmas for media studies. In cases where an SVOD is the only access to the content, titles become characteristic of different logics than those that have supported movies and television. This creates conceptual confusion that might be insignificant semantics: do we call *Stranger Things* a television series, or maybe just a 'series'? In other cases, they become matters of notable consequence for award eligibility and within hierarchies perceived by creators: see debates surrounding Oscar and film festival eligibility.

Although some Hollywood directors have quite passionately argued for the distinction of movies as defined by theatrical screening, we must begin the act of categorizing by understanding why the categorization is being done and how it is helpful to bringing a particular phenomenon into relief. Just as viewers' experience of SVODs as being much like television services isn't paramount to understanding how these services work as businesses, neither are the feelings of directors. From a *media industries perspective*, the lens through which this book approaches SVODs, it is not clear that, in 2022, 'movie' and 'television series' remain *industrial subcategories* with nearly the usefulness as was once the case, though they are of course tremendously useful categories of story type. In other words, even though *as viewers* we still understand there to be a difference between series and movies, I'd suggest we're hard put to explain that distinction as consistently anything other than run-time. Those of *us who study media* do recognize differences, although they are diminishing, and there may be greater industrial similarity between some types of series and movie production than across all movies or all series. Suggesting diminished industrial distinction between series and movies doesn't negate the existence or history of differences once more pronounced. Rather, it helps open us to identifying what categories of video do provide significant distinctions that enable us to better theorize the various markets and submarkets that now exist because there is more meaningful consistency across the categories.

Movies and the series most pervasive on general SVODs have similar underlying economic characteristics in terms of their high cost of production and their enduring value as public goods (in economic terms). Rather than classify video based on what screen or distribution technology once characterized its norms or its run-time, the more substantive determinants of commercial video characteristics in the current ecosystem are whether they are funded by a service seeking subscriber dollars or attention for advertisers and whether they are offered in the marketplace as single goods or bundled libraries. SVODs introduce a variety of changes in business norms, particularly that their commissioned series and films aren't intended to pass through multiple distribution windows to earn value. In 2022, ad-funded versus subscriber-funded versus transaction video are more compelling ways to organize the universe of scripted fiction video than movie versus series, at least for industrial analysis.[10]

Just as the technology, industrial formations, government policies, and viewing practices of film and television have evolved over their existence, the practices of SVODs are neither static nor uniform. For example, few SVODs commission content, and, among those that do, the type of content prioritized varies considerably. Similarly, simple narratives of video-service succession that suggest broadcasting previously dominated video distribution to the home and that internet distribution will come to *replace* it are limiting. Instead, we might imagine an extended period in which many norms of video delivery and video businesses coexist given their particular affordances without any one category of service eliminating others.

SVODs share the provision of video in common with previous technologies. The experience of the libraries they curate bear semblance to video rental stores, and their subscriber funding makes purely subscriber-funded channels such as HBO and Showtime precedents. We may watch them on the same screens used to view many other types of video and we may use their stories for the same cultural purposes for which we've used television and movies, but, industrially, SVODs are different in ways that explain the emerging differences in what stories they tell and what motivates their telling. The first part of the book explores those differences in order to identify their basis and why they matter to how we understand SVODs and their role in culture and media economies.

Key terms

Just as SVOD has been selected for its precision, here are some key terms that appear throughout the book with explanation of how and why they are used in particular ways.

Internet-distributed video

Internet-distributed video is a technological category based on the use of internet protocol technologies to distribute, or 'stream', video. SVODs are one sector of internet-distributed video. The claims made here are not true of all internet-distributed video – which would include many more services, such as AVODs and the video supplied by social media services – because the revenue model leads to very different strategies and priorities. The book most frequently uses terminology of video instead of television or movies because most services offer both and treat them indiscriminately.

Commission

Commissions are series and movies that SVODs 'create' (confusingly and imprecisely also called 'originals' by the services). 'Create' doesn't mean self-produce, but commissions are titles for which the SVOD pays a substantial amount of production cost that allows it a more direct curatorial role in determining the content and tone of programming associated with the service and also to have input on the production. Commissions can be produced by a production company owned by the SVOD or by others; commissions are not necessarily produced 'in-house' (meaning a production company owned by the SVOD or an entity that owns the SVOD and production company).

The point of establishing language that distinguishes commissioned and licensed content – or titles initially created by or for another service – is to identify particular industrial conditions that have implications for what stories are told and how they are told, not to create an inflexible typology. Relatively few SVODs commission content – especially scripted fiction – at this point, but it is the opportunity to create with the specific industrial logics of SVODs guiding them that introduces some of the greatest rupture with past thinking and understanding of industrial limitations on the creation of culture.

There are many peculiarities that blur these classifications. With series, generally the question of 'where did it first air?' can be asked to identify the commissioner, although this can be obscured in cases where content is created outside one's country. *Co-commissions* are similar to commissions but are developed jointly with another entity that also receives first-window distribution, typically a broadcast channel that secures initial linear national rights to a series. To date, this has been used most extensively by Netflix, which buys rights to offer the series in all its other national libraries, and often it also becomes available in the national library of the co-commissioning broadcaster's country after a year.

As of February 2020, co-commissions accounted for 24 per cent of Netflix scripted commissions.[11] Owners of several SVODs (Peacock, HBO Max, and Disney+) also own linear ad-supported services. At this early stage of development, it is unclear whether titles simultaneously distributed through both linear and SVOD services should be classified as co-commissions.

The category of 'commission' is more difficult for movies because of the legacy of theatrical distribution. To be clear, the reason to make a distinction is because we would expect commissions to provide the purest articulation of content strategy, followed by co-commissions, then licensed content. The purpose of this categorization is to recognize underlying industrial distinctions and appropriately group cases; it is not evaluative. In the case of owned-IP SVODs (Disney+, HBO Max, Paramount+), I would argue movies created with the intention of non-exclusive SVOD play should not be considered as commissions; however, I would consider movies funded by Netflix that receive limited theatrical screening as commissions because, while the theatrical revenue is a business motivation of the owned-IP SVODs, this is not the case for Netflix.[12] This distinction became particularly complicated for movies during the COVID-19 pandemic. *Mulan*, *Soul*, and *Hamilton* were not intended as Disney+ commissions but appeared as such due to cinema closures (similar for Warner Bros.' 2021 slate in the US, but many of these day-and-date US HBO Max titles received an exclusive theatrical window outside the US). With COVID-19 operating as an intervening variable, it is not yet clear how theatrically distributed films fit into the offerings of owned-IP SVODs.

Most SVOD libraries are full of titles that were commissioned by another entity – usually a channel somewhere around the world or a movie made for theatrical distribution – and the SVOD pays to license rights to offer the title. There are two different categories of licensing: regular and exclusive. Exclusive licensing typically costs more because there is added value in being the only place to access content, especially for subscriber-funded services (thus, price-sensitive viewers cannot simply 'wait' for a title to show up on an ad-supported service). Often SVODs buy the right to be the only outlet for the programme in a country; sometimes they just buy exclusive rights among other SVODs.

Again, the key reason to distinguish between commissioned and licensed titles is that commissions allow the purest sense of SVOD content strategy. Of course, licensed titles can do this work too, especially for services that license strategically for the SVOD service rather than just offering owned IP. But much of SVODs' strategy is built on offering a subtle distinction from existing linear services. Relying on content created for another service – unless created in another territory – limits that distinction. The differences between series and movies again leads to some discrepancies. Some movies were developed without SVOD funding or input but then acquired by an SVOD with no or limited theatrical release (for example, *Beasts of No Nation*, *Roma*, *Wolfwalkers*). I use the term 'global acquisition' from Christopher Meir to distinguish such films.[13] Several non-US films receive exclusive distribution outside their country in this way and straddle the commissioned versus licensed dichotomy. On one hand, these titles offer considerable value to an SVOD as exclusive titles, although the SVOD does not have the opportunity to develop these titles in a manner optimized to its content strategy. But, again, the SVOD acquires a known good – a completed film, not a concept for a film – and can accordingly assess its value and relevance to strategy.

The dynamics of commissioning work differently for services without a pre-existing library of IP (Netflix, Amazon, Apple) than for those based on owned IP (Disney+, HBO Max, Paramount+). A decade from now, we'll have the evidence needed to examine the distinctiveness of series and movies commissioned by owned-IP SVODs. In the short term, the latter will be strongly defined by the access that they provide to a haphazard collection of titles. Part II features a more extensive discussion of Netflix's commissioning and licensing.

Linear v. non-linear/on demand
There is nothing unusual about the use of 'linear' in this book, it is just not a common term. Linear denotes the organization of video content in a schedule such that one show follows another. It is used here to describe what has long been 'normal' for television and in contrast to the on-demand capability of SVODs.

Content
Some take offence at calling movies and series 'content,' suggesting the word evacuates their artistic and cultural merit. I offer my apologies to those with such beliefs, but content is a convenient term for generally referencing the video made available by SVODs, whether created originally for television channels, theatrical release, or particularly for an SVOD service.

Scripted fiction
The SVODs examined here mostly offer scripted fiction content, and occasionally this analysis focuses on

scripted fiction – or conventional comedy and drama movies and series. The reason for this focus is that the cost of such forms is typically higher than other formats that might be commissioned. Thus, it means something more substantial for an SVOD to commission twenty scripted series or movies than twenty stand-up comedy specials. Scripted fiction is not the best term because obviously stand-up specials and documentaries too are 'scripted' and 'narrative' (another alternative word that doesn't really solve the problem), but we lack more precise terminology. Again, the point is why the analysis here makes distinctions among different kinds of content. It is never evaluative but always in an effort to 'compare apples with apples'.

Distribution windows

A key norm of audiovisual industries before SVODs was the practice of making content available through different distribution technologies, in different places, for a period of time. For example, a Hollywood movie would first be available in a cinema, and then on aeroplanes, DVD, premium cable (HBO), basic cable, and broadcast television. Each of these is a window, and these windows might be mixed with coterminous or varied distribution windows in different countries as well.

This practice of using tiered release through techno-logical, temporal, and geographic windows emerged in response to some of the peculiar industrial dynamics of media goods relative to other goods. Television and movies are 'public goods', an economic classification for goods to denote how one person's consumption does not use them up. This attribute, in combination with the lack of marginal cost, leads increasing scale to be a particular priority in commercial media industries. Before on-demand access was technologically feasible, video industries relied on windowing to maximize revenue from content. Windowing enabled the creation of artificial scarcity in support of price discrimination used to derive as much profit as possible from media goods. Thus movies were first available only in the environment that would allow the greatest per person revenue. Certainly, many consumers recognized this and chose to wait for content to reach the window with the price that matched the value proposition provided to them. The system was designed to try to compel higher payment from those so eager to access content they would pay more not to wait.

At first, SVODs were assumed to be another window for content, and, in many cases of licensed content, this remains the dynamic. But over the last decade SVODs have become commissioners and thus initiators of programming. A key difference they have introduced to strategy is to hold their content in relative perpetuity rather than allowing it to proceed through various windows.[14] This strategy is related to the revenue model. If content created by SVODs will later become available without subscription cost, it reduces the incentive to subscribe. Also, the on-demand environment (as well as subscriber funding) enables services to derive value whenever subscribers encounter content; it need not be at a prescribed time, as needed in the case of selling attention to advertisers.

But-what-about? critiques
As much as I've tried to delineate rules and distinctions, I know nearly all have the odd exception. If I listed every peripheral counter-example it would be difficult to build

the 'generally' or 'mostly' true claims that do allow us the conceptual clarity to advance thinking in this area. So yes, for example, Netflix occasionally releases some titles in theatres, has licensed a few titles to linear channels, earns a very small amount from some advertising deals, is launching a consumer goods business connected to its titles, and is experimenting with a linear offering, but none of this erodes the dominant norms of the service as of 2022 as a pure play, subscriber-funded, video-on-demand service. Likewise, services noted as 'predominantly' owned IP will simply be referenced as owned IP throughout.

PART I

Subscriber-Funded Streaming Services are Different from Linear Services

1
Experience: On Schedules and Viewing Practices

Almost all commentary about SVODs begins and ends with discussion of their content library and programmes. This focus misses a key way in which SVODs differ from linear services. I'm not suggesting that content is unimportant but, rather, asserting that experience strongly moderates the value proposition a service offers and distinguishes SVODs significantly from linear and AVOD alternatives. The role of experience in understanding the contemporary video ecosystem is something like: *Content × Experience = Value Proposition.*

It makes sense that experience has been overlooked. Experience has not been a factor in viewing practice in the past because it has been largely constant. Perhaps, with the exception of Raymond Williams's attention to 'flow' in *Television: Technology and Cultural Form*, we didn't think much about there being profoundly different experiences of television, because there weren't. In much of the world, for as long as most can remember, television shows were delivered according to a schedule.

There were often regular commercial breaks, and new episodes of a show became available weekly – or daily – and so on. There is nothing natural about those norms; they are not inherent to 'television'. They simply emerged based on the opportunities and limitations of the first technologies capable of distributing video to the home and in response to the metrics of success that dictated their funding.

But experience matters now. We are increasingly familiar with talk of 'user experience' in relation to websites and apps, but SVOD experience is much more than interface ease of use.

First, there is the experiential gulf between *linear* and *on demand*. Neither is simply 'better' or 'worse'; rather, they are differently suited for different revenue models and programme features, and they encourage different cultural experiences. The variable amount of choice that linear and on-demand services offer leads to different decision-making processes and viewing behaviours: seeking particular content, perusing a particular library, or the more spontaneous simplicity of electing 'what's on'. We don't know much about how viewers regard any of these experiences. There is little research suggesting whether typical patterns exist among viewers, if there are particular typologies of behaviour, or whether there is considerable variation just at the individual level. There are complicated and intentional choices being made, even if they are made subconsciously.

Another aspect of experience that tends to align with the distinction of linear versus on demand is whether or not content is interrupted by commercials. Of course many publicly funded linear services don't have advertising, nor do purely subscriber-funded channels such as HBO (at least in the US), but most linear

Experience

television has been dominated by ad-funding and the interruption of commercial messages. Hence another experiential difference involves whether the experience includes spending as much as a quarter of every hour occupied with advertisements or whether viewers are able to watch only the sought-after content – albeit at a monetary cost – using SVOD services.

In the case of video divided into segments – or what we have known as 'episodes' – another significant experiential dimension relates to the extent to which different types of services allow viewers access to those segments. There are notable experiential differences to being able to access only *a recent episode, the current season, or all the episodes of a title.* Notably, simply having full access to all the episodes does not require a viewer to watch them a particular way; it simply supplies the choice.

Next is a question of *library stability.* To what extent can a subscriber rely on favourite titles or those of interest to remain available? Library stability allows viewers to follow the whim of impulse with no need to worry about watching something before it is 'gone'. After these considerations, experience might be evaluated in terms of the ease of *interface negotiation, recommendation,* and *search capabilities.* And, finally, attributes such as the ease of *starting the next episode,* of easily *restarting* wherever viewing stopped, and perhaps of the service remembering the last point of viewing *across multiple devices* all enhance viewer experience.

Despite the attention given to different shows or intellectual property controlled by different companies, or to buzzy announcements of certain stars or creators aligning with particular services, it is possible to imagine that a high-quality experience trumps content. Or at least that experience contributes strongly to driving viewers between linear, AVOD, and SVOD contexts. Personally, I cannot tolerate commercials. I would rather not watch television or film than sit through content with commercials. I know such an extreme example is not normal, but it illustrates how experience can structure the universe of viewing choices. I will choose content I'd rate as B or B+ over A or A– if there are experience hurdles to the A content. (Though A+ content is worth the hurdles; to be clear, these 'grades' are based on my personal taste profile and not universal content ratings).

Experience can become a factor at many moments in the viewing process; this is often called 'friction' when people write about technology use. A telling illustration was how little Amazon Prime Video I watched until it became available on the Apple TV (the device I used to connect my television to the internet). I knew how to use Airplay to throw the content from my phone to the living room screen, but I rarely did it. The hassle of its burning through battery or that I wasn't able to be simultaneously on my phone made it too 'inconvenient' relative to my desire to watch the content available on Amazon. Then, one day, there was an Amazon Prime Video app at the top of the Apple TV menu, and we watched nothing but Amazon Prime Video for a few weeks.

Moving across the world from the US to Australia a few years ago required buying all new electronics and encountering a mostly new video ecosystem (except for Netflix and Amazon, though the libraries aren't precisely the same) and a whole new universe of shows. Everything was made strange, and this made differences in experience particularly clear. Sometimes

Experience

I wanted to watch a series on ABC iView (Australia's publicly funded broadcaster's ad-free catch-up service), but the thought of negotiating its interface was 'too hard' (because I found it counter-intuitive, and I often struggled to find content I knew was available) when I could watch the next episode of *Money Heist* on Netflix with one click. Also, I knew that, once one episode was over, I'd be returned to the home screen to repeat the byzantine process of finding the show rather than be easily ushered to the next episode. Or I generally avoided the AVODs because I repeatedly had the experience of content freezing during commercials (so nothing happened for the first minute of a three-minute commercial block, making the disruption four minutes or longer), or of the freeze never ending, kicking me back to a home screen and forcing me to start the episode from the beginning (or fast forward to where I left off, but replaying every commercial break); in short, a horrible experience. I may be uncommonly impatient, but these anecdotes illustrate how experience factors into the current video ecosystem and the kinds of choices viewers make, mostly without recognizing they make them at all.

My viewing behaviour may not fit the norm, but it is difficult to know what is normal these days. For some viewers – in particular those who study and work in video industries – content might deserve the unbridled supremacy indicated by endless talk of shows and libraries as key to streaming service success. But the psychographic that writes about video industries isn't representative of the general population of viewers. Also difference in experience is difficult to quantify, and we lack necessary concepts and terminology – remember, we are still using 'binge viewing' to talk about everything that isn't watched on a linear schedule.[1] There is much to say about SVOD content, but this discussion intentionally begins by putting experience on the table.

Too many discussions – especially those that compare SVODs with linear ad-supported channels – speak only of content and ignore the difference in experience. Such a frame neglects the variation in value proposition that derives from the distinctive revenue model, technological affordances, and business strategies of SVODs. People pay for SVODs because of the content, but also to access the experience. Not all SVODs offer an equivalent experience, and there is a universe of difference between AVOD catch-up services and SVODs, even though both are internet distributed. Experience might not be relevant to all questions and analysis, but it is crucial to many and far too rarely acknowledged.

Hegemony of linear norms

A key differentiation of SVODs from linear services is the availability of content on demand instead of on a schedule. This enables the experience of video content in a manner more akin to other forms of media such as print and music that have been readily available for users to consume on their own schedule or at their own chosen pace. No one has argued that listening to music on the radio is the 'right' way or that there is something untoward about listening to an entire album from start to finish. Oddly, reading a book in one sitting is regarded as indicative of high praise, while viewing a series on SVODs at a self-determined schedule has led to criticism of 'binging' a series, although the pathological components of that term are not always intended.

Experience

These internalized biases towards experiencing video on a schedule reveal the *hegemony of linear norms*. We tend to prioritize the existing norm, and that prevents us from recognizing how on-demand video services are strongly differentiated from those bound to a linear schedule. Here I use 'hegemony' to mean a predominant or a pervasive manner of thinking. It refers to the means by which certain ideas come to seem so normal we can't imagine them being any other way. We don't even realize there are alternatives, that there could be another way, because these assumptions of what is 'normal' are so deeply integrated into our worldview.

The hegemony of linear norms includes most all the things we think about television, how we assume 'television' to be – or should be – that tie back to our long experience of it as delivered by a schedule (here the 'we' is probably people born before 2000). None of those norms are inherent to 'television'. They are strategies that developed over time – mostly before anyone around now remembers – and relate to the capabilities of television's first distribution technology: broadcasting. Being freed from linear norms encourages different delivery strategies (such as dropping a bunch of episodes at once) and content strategies (such as offering titles passionately loved by a segment of subscribers, because titles can be 'successful' even if they don't attract a mass audience).

Broadcasting can send only a single signal at a time. It is built into the technology, and it is an amazing technology for sharing a single message with a mass audience simultaneously. If you can transmit only one thing at a time, you choose your programming in a particular way. In an advertiser-funded system, which is predominantly the case for linear television, channels try to schedule the item that most people will like at a time when most people are watching. A public-service, public-funded system might instead air the programming believed most important to the citizenry during peak viewing hours – but audience size is commonly the most readily identifiable metric for these systems as well (though it should not be so prioritized). Many linear norms related to scheduling derive from the fact that the core business is not – as viewers think – entertaining and informing them but, rather, assembling the attention of those viewers in order to sell it to advertisers. The concept of 'prime time' is not ordained by deity, it is simply strategic. Advertiser-funded television is foremost about using programming to make an audience.

These linear norms of assembling an audience are baked into nearly all assumptions and understandings of how television works, and they are so deeply embedded we forget there are alternatives. But SVODs aren't linear or ad-funded and don't have to follow these norms. Their ability to serve up programming on demand and to pursue programmes that audiences will pay to access rather than those that will attract the most attention make them profoundly different from 'television channels'.

The ability to deliver programming on demand radically shifts priorities and the strategies available for serving audiences. Crucially, SVODs are not trying to make a singular audience. Linear television is all about building and maintaining the attention of a mass of viewers around a single programme – of choosing among scores of shows and trying to divine which one will attract the most viewers. But, for SVODs, it's a matter of 'yes, and'. On demand allows a service to offer many different things simultaneously, and it matters little where or when that audience accumulates. Instead of building *an* audience, on-demand delivery allows SVODs to build audience*s*, and it is amazing what a difference that plural 's' can make: it completely changes the calculus of programming. Notably, this is a function of both the subscriber funding and the on-demand attributes of SVODs – in combination they redefine the business significantly.

The viability of loved by some

The ability to serve individuals, rather than needing to adhere to the mandate to make a singular audience, dethrones 'least objectionable' as a core strategy of media distribution with scarcity limits. 'Least objectionable' is the term that emerged in the US system to explain commercial networks' programming strategy in the years of competition among three channels.[2] It is well suited to a context of limited choice and addresses how the three US networks selected programmes and how audiences – often families or couples – more likely chose the show that was 'least objectionable' than one any member particularly liked. One person might most want choice A and the other choice B. Choice C offers neither's preference but the second choice of both, making it 'least objectionable'. This strategy illustrates how the competitive conditions at the time did not reward developing shows towards which a segment of the audience might be particularly passionate. The attributes that attracted the passion of some likely discouraged others from viewing. A version of 'least objectionable' also might explain Hollywood studios' support of films likely to be acceptable to 'all four quadrants' (male/female, young/old) with resources likely to make them 'blockbusters', even if few of these titles become 'favourite' films.

Although 'least objectionable' programming has been a less viable strategy for some time – at least on television systems with scores of channels – it is crucial to recall this context. In contrast, subscriber funding and on-demand delivery encourage services to be many things to many people or to offer content aimed at particular passions. Rather than 'least objectionable', SVODs' model encourages them to aim for 'loved by some'. (Of course they'd like to achieve 'loved by all', but that isn't how taste works most of the time.)

Viewers expect different things from SVODs. They aren't likely to leave them on from sun up to sun down the way they leave a television tuned to a linear channel. Instead, SVODs build their business by being a reliable source for a couple of hours of drama, comedy, or a provocative documentary at the end of a workday. Their business model requires they offer content a bit different from those 'broad' enough to amass the audience scale needed by a linear ad-supported channel, although the experience they offer may alone be enough to motivate monthly payment. Their distribution technology allows them to cater to specific interests with a multiplicity of titles available on demand rather than attempt to be 'least objectionable' to the most viewers.

Television's linear origin imposed time specificity as a crucial feature. Most measures of success are time based: did the show win its timeslot; how many people are watching at the time an advertisement appears? Or, in theatrical distribution, what was the opening weekend box office? It is delightfully straightforward. But how do you measure success when time doesn't

matter? Or, more radically, if it doesn't matt
people watch, and a service offers a library of opt
does it even matter what they watch? Not really – jus
that they watch or, rather, that they find enough to
watch that they feel their fee is warranted.

The hegemony of linear norms leads to a lot of
misunderstanding of SVODs. It leads us to assume
many of the 'truths' of television should be applied.
When SVODs started dropping all episodes simultaneously, the traditional industry responded with complete
disbelief: 'What novices these guys are! They have no
idea how to build or maintain an audience.' But SVODs'
priority isn't building an audience, at least in the sense
of getting viewers to show up at a particular time over
a period of months. Despite years of this norm, critique
of the full season drop comes back at times, often in
conversations about how SVODs would be 'smarter' to
milk the buzz of new titles for longer. Or some perplex-
ingly assert that viewers' experience would be better if
they were required to wait between episodes. Clearly,
if subscribers think that is the case, they can pace their
viewing; on-demand delivery allows that choice. But
imposing weekly releases risks degrading the experience
for others, and that risks dissatisfaction, and dissatisfaction risks churn (cancelling the service). Preventing
dissatisfaction is more important than attracting a big
audience to any title at any one time.

The hegemony of linear thinking may offer 'truths' of
linear ad-supported channels, but such truths offer poor
guidance to a service that succeeds by satisfying viewers.
An SVOD's fundamental objective is not maximizing
the audience for a title; it is maximizing the satisfaction
of its subscribers, which leads it to prioritize providing
the desired experience. The ability to serve a multiplicity

of tastes also allows strategies different from those that produce a singular mass audience.

Titles in an SVOD library provide value to the service whenever viewers find the title: in a week, in a month, or years later. Of course, SVODs seek efficiency in content spending and to find the equilibrium whereby they can maintain the maximum number of viewers with the fewest titles (unless they own the titles). But it is more valuable for SVODs to offer an excellent experience, emphasize developing distinctive content for subscribers, and make sure viewers can find that content than play at the game of attracting mass audience attention.

Make me feel_____

Once viewers move from an environment that involves choosing only among what is showing on a particular night – either on TV or at the cinema – to the depth of options offered by SVOD libraries, content selection can be more purposive rather than a matter of the 'least objectionable' option. Entirely new viewing behaviours and practices become possible, and it is easier for viewers to choose content to achieve a certain end, such as retreat into silly comedy, get lost in an intense drama, or investigate that show a co-worker told them about. New viewing practices are enabled by the *availability* (on-demand libraries with many choices) and *reliability* (you don't have to watch it now or it's gone) of SVODs. Such viewing practices are nascent, and have barely been examined, but are important considerations for those designing SVOD library strategies.

Experience

Netflix's VP of Product, Todd Yellin, claims that people seek out stories for three different reasons – to escape, to expand their horizons, or to be able to share in the 'what everyone is talking about' conversation.[3] 'Escape' likely has a lot of different dimensions, and, in thinking of some of my own recent choices, it is often a fine line between seeking to escape and seeking to expand my horizons. Yellin is probably simplifying, but his comments are provocative and raise the question of whether the difference in SVOD experience might also allow new viewing practices.

In facing the scale of choice offered by an SVOD library, viewers are better able to make selections aimed at producing a desired state of being – horror will scare us; a thriller will excite; a romantic comedy might leave us warm and hopeful. The abundance and diversity of content increasingly available in SVOD libraries enables viewers to engage in a broader range of mood management, though our selection of content to achieve certain mood states may be fully unintentional. For example, when I choose a raunchy mom-com, maybe it is because I'm a bit frustrated and lonely and want something in which I can identify familiar struggle. When I watch *Madam Secretary* or *Borgen*, it is similar, but more an underlying desire for inspiration or encouragement rather than laughter. Of course a lot of the time the selection is plainer: I need a movie that my tweenagers will tolerate that won't make me want to poke my eyes out. I don't care what it is 'about', just that it lets us enjoy sharing time together.

We have very rarely talked about broadcast television programming in terms of how it makes us feel. I've read many accounts of programme scheduling strategy, why networks select certain shows, and the characteristics

41

perceived to make them valuable, and I can't think of an instance in which anything like this was mentioned. There is a trajectory of media research called 'uses and gratifications' that examines how people use media to achieve different ends. The trouble is that the television of the time at which uses and gratifications was at its peak – in the 1970s and 1980s – really wasn't all that different.[4] The whole pursuit of 'least objectionable' programming led most content to fall into Yellin's general category of 'escape'. If the three US commercial networks were counterprogramming one another, you might find a choice between a drama, a comedy, and a news magazine, but all would be trying to appeal broadly. Importantly, as more of a sociological than a film/screen studies theory, uses and gratifications did allow for the use of television out of habit, companionship, and passing the time – in other words, reasons separate from attitude towards the content being watched. These motivations reflect the dynamics of broadcast norms.

Writing this account reminds me of the hours I spent in the aisles of video rental stores as a teen trying to figure out what to rent. For many, the video rental store was the first experience of wide-ranging video choice. The expanse of possibility held on those shelves! I didn't realize it at the time, but those selections were often driven by a desire to feel a certain way. And that experience is more like choosing among SVOD libraries than ever the case of linear television. Even with hundreds of channels, all those channels sought the viewing mass and planed off a lot of edgy content to do so.

The scarcity of analogue-era video constrained the ability to use media for mood management or to service a substantial range of sensibilities, which led to using content features – genres or categories such as sports or news – to characterize video. Television and movies devised a set of programme categories based on attributes of story, characters, casting, and genre. These attributes allowed us to sort features of the content, and they functioned somewhat as proxies for what we wanted to feel in viewing. But amid today's viewing choice, our selections may be better understood by investigating how we select stories to make us feel a certain way.

The different industrial characteristics of SVODs warrant asking questions such as why people watch and how they select among known choices as well as initially. SVODs allow new ways of offering content and a greater array of content, and these attributes likely change viewer processes of selection. And, importantly, SVODs' on-demand capacity allows them to serve various desires, not just those perceived to be the most common. There is valuable research to be done about these processes – do people want certain content or do they want a particular experience? It is probably a mix of these. Maybe there are typologies of viewers; maybe all viewers seek a mix.

It is necessary to ask these questions and imagine that there are different processes involved in viewers' selection of SVOD content, and there may be very different ways to categorize content. Here, too, we see evidence of a hegemony, a particular lens of understanding and vocabulary that we've brought with us from other ways of distributing video. But focusing on what content is about may not be the most useful language for conceptualizing the SVOD environment.

2
Building Libraries: Conglomerating Niches and Beyond?

SVODs arguably pursue content strategies never before feasible. Not because they figured out something new, but because building a library is different than building a schedule. This simple sentence introduces a concept not previously central to discussion of video services – *library*. Most of our language for organizing video derives from linear ad-supported television, which also spoke of programmes or titles but conceived of them primarily in terms of a *schedule* and developed an expansive vocabulary related to scheduling practices. Broadcasters selected programmes to fit a schedule that would maintain viewers across the night and used strategies such as hammocking, tent-poles, and lead-ins to encourage a viewer to tune in and stay. Hollywood studios focused on managing a *slate* and relied on release strategies that would maximize box-office audiences and minimize competition. For SVODs, 'library' is the key term for the oeuvre of offerings.

44

As discussed, the basis of building a schedule – especially for an ad-funded service – is trying to attract a mass of viewers. By this logic, a good library would be one that had the most people reading the same book – not at all an appropriate measure. Rather, a commercial library might be regarded as successful because it serves the interests of many different people by offering many types of content (general library), or it may derive value by offering extraordinary depth in a particular type of content (specific library).[1]

In discussing media audiences, the word 'niche' is a common antonym to 'mass' and a way to speak of media fragmentation. Sometimes it connotes content of very narrow or peculiar value, and perhaps 'segment' is less value laden. But, regardless of the word used, the point is that the library often gains value by offering segments of content attractive to different viewer preferences because subscribers can access any part of the library on demand.

Niches and segments have been contrary to linear video businesses because their smaller and specific audience scope limits a service from achieving economies of scale. But SVODs, particularly those offering a general library, can achieve scale by providing content for multiple segments at once. Instead of operating as a *one-auditorium theatre*, as is characteristic of linear services that aim to construct a large audience for a single show, SVODs can operate as a *many-roomed library* that offers a range content rather than driving toward the least objectionable. This strategy is enabled by distribution technology; SVODs are not limited to delivering a particular piece of content at a scheduled time. Subscribers have entry to the library in its entirety, though in practice they may only ever visit a single room, and perhaps only a single shelf in that room. For example, the Netflix content that shapes my experience and perception of the service may not overlap at all with that of my neighbour, and my preferred 'shelf' of its library no more defines the service than does his. (This metaphor is made slippery by the use of recommendation algorithms that direct my neighbour and me to different options. This is discussed in chapter 4.)

In 2017, in *Portals*, I described this as a 'conglomerated niche' strategy as a way to make sense of the distinction I saw emerging from Netflix. It remains early days for other general global SVODs, but the others – likely due to their reliance on owned IP – have yet to offer evidence of a library strategy particularly befitting the characteristics of SVODs. In some ways SVODs with general libraries paradoxically can blend the two strategies typical of television competition before their arrival: *mass scale* of broadcasting and *niche segmentation* of cable/satellite channels. The ability to provide on-demand access enables SVODs to execute this distinctive strategy of servicing multiple tastes and sensibilities simultaneously, and transnational services achieve scale by serving segments on a transnational basis.

Such a strategy both mirrors and runs counter to those of niche cable and broadcast channels, so that this segmentation strategy is not entirely without precedent. In many ways, the conglomeration of the US television industry in the 1990s aimed to produce a version of a conglomerated niche strategy with the available delivery technology of the time. In amassing ownership of a range of cable channels, including Nickelodeon, MTV, VH1, TV Land, and Comedy Central – as well as with mass-targeted broadcast network CBS

– Viacom (particularly as it was constituted from 1999 to 2005) set a precedent for this segmentation strategy by combining multiple niche, linear-delivered, nationally bound programme services. Similar examples can be found on cable and satellite systems around the globe, as can many of the Viacom channels. By the start of the twenty-first century, most cable channels in the US and globally sought a clear brand identity and to schedule programmes that reinforced branding done through marketing and promotion. To some degree, the success of these channels could be measured by the popular awareness of the brand; branding became crucial as multichannel competition became robust, and channels needed to differentiate and communicate a clear identity to stand out as the options for viewers grew.[2] But, in most cases, these specific brands needed the scale of being part of a suite of channels to be viable.

These separate channels in some ways mirror the 'verticals' – or categories of content – that SVODs with general libraries can develop in a many-roomed library. Though compelling claims about the programming of particular niches could be made about individual channels such as Nickelodeon, MTV, and even a more general broadcaster such as CBS, no one would have considered making either a brand claim about the whole of Viacom's programming or a common assessment of the 'quality' or accomplishment of its content. General-library SVODs defy single brand claims but can articulate multiple content-based value propositions or features. For instance, Netflix has no singular content brand, and its library strategy is investigated in depth in chapter 8. It remains to be seen whether the owned-IP SVODs will tailor their identity through particular content segments in their commissioning strategy. Disney+ has made steps in this direction by using Marvel and Star Wars IP as verticals of development, and its National Geographic and the children's and family brand with which the company is most closely associated suggest possible other segments it may service.

As a result of the different logics of programming for a many-roomed library, SVOD subscribers might describe a programming brand that correlates with their own viewing, even if library breadth and the aim of conglomerating niches defies a single brand identity and even enables outright contradiction. The audience scale an SVOD can achieve with a general library cannot be understood as following a 'broadcast' strategy. Broadcasting seeks the opposite of the segment; it is the effort to identify programming widely acceptable to – though likely not deeply desired by – the largest number of viewers.

The other precedent for the conglomerated niche strategy of some SVODs is the US subscriber-funded cable channel HBO, which similarly relies entirely on subscribers for revenue. HBO too conglomerates niches, but the limitations of linear distribution enabled much less scale in terms of content – so less discernible segmenting. For much of its history, HBO served audiences that sought content otherwise unavailable on television: movies without content editing or commercials reasonably soon after theatrical release, niche sports, and content too edgy for broadcast or basic cable's nervous advertisers and content restrictions. Certainly, some viewers may have watched bits of all these programme types, but it is just as likely that access to any one segment of this otherwise exclusive programming drove subscription. Eventually HBO commissioned original scripted content: first movies that were acclaimed and distinctive from the movies produced for theatrical release or 'made-for' television, and then series likewise distinctive from television commissioned by broadcasters. HBO was able to establish a reputation for programme excellence based on those movies and series, although the critically discussed titles are only a subset of its commissions, and other titles served other niches.

Commissioning bespoke content allows an SVOD the most precise cultivation of a library strategy but is also an expensive and risky endeavour and infeasible for many SVODs. The inability to commission content isn't a terrible limitation; it just means that many services create value primarily by facilitating an experience otherwise unavailable by improving access to titles. But as of 2022, most of the content available for licensing was produced with the goal of attracting mass audiences. This limits the value of the content to an SVOD's efforts to offer a distinctive value proposition. This is also the limit faced by SVODs with owned-IP libraries, since that IP was created to meet the programme needs of video services with different business models, brands, and programme strategies. As a result, there is less differentiation among owned-IP SVOD strategies and previous forms of distribution than for Netflix at the library level.

Amassing commissioned content may one day lead Netflix to own most of its offerings in the manner currently characteristic of the predominantly owned-IP SVODs, but a crucial distinction will remain that all of Netflix's IP was commissioned specifically for its streaming service. Thus, where the owned-IP services have thousands of hours of content they have created for theatrical release or a wide range of television channels – content thus developed with very different programming logics than those that distinguish SVODs – Netflix's content development has always been in the service of its subscriber-funded offering.

To be clear, the general library and segmenting of audience are deliberate content strategies and not required by distribution technology – though they align well to subscriber funding and on-demand delivery. They also aren't the only strategies available to SVODs. Other SVODs seek market share by offering considerable depth in one niche – such as Crunchyroll as an anime service, Acorn with its particular brand of mystery and thriller, or discovery+ with its library of factual entertainment originally created for HGTV, Food Network, Animal Planet, and the Travel and Discovery channels. And, in truth, the owned-IP services such as Disney+, HBO Max, Paramount+, and Hulu are using SVODs primarily to distribute content made for other services and markets and thus are 'general' more by accident than through strategy.

Libraries are quite different from linear television schedules in the clues they provide about viewer experience. The scarcity of the schedule gives each programme in it a level of importance – slots in the schedule are scarce and finite – but not every title in a library warrants the same degree of importance. And where time of day indicates information about the relative importance of a programme in a schedule, there is no equivalent in an on-demand library delivered via personalized interface. Moreover, the variation or similarity of libraries for a single service across different countries tells us very little about what people in different places actually watch with certainty.

The ability to service multiple audiences simultaneously by being no one thing is crucial to appreciating the content strategies available to SVODs at a macro level. It is also the root explanation for why SVODs can thrive while developing content that would not be made for a linear ad-supported context due to expectation it would fail to achieve the broad attention necessary. This also suggests why it is more apt to compare SVODs to a video rental store than to a linear ad-supported channel. Though many movies in the rental store were designed to drive a broad audience to the box office, the video rental store was also a place that offered access to movies that never received broad theatrical distribution. The key to the success of an SVOD need not be based on building mass interest behind a few titles. Such a strategy is more economically efficient, but it is also not how the economics of media tastes work. Creating content special enough that people will pay to access it requires offering something worth paying for.

SVOD library strategies can differ from linear ad-supported channel strategies, as well as from those designed to drive box-office attendance. Figuring out viable library strategies will determine the field of services that survive. The question I think I've been asked by every journalist I've talked to in the last five years is 'How many services will people subscribe to?' It is an impossible question; the answer can only be 'it depends'. Do you have a car? Two? Do you also have a bike? Do you also walk places? Take public transport? *The number of SVOD services people will pay for depends on what these services offer and individuals' video needs, desires, and discretionary spending.* This is not the same situation as enticing viewers to a channel to which they already have access, as was the case for FX and AMC fighting their way into the American mainstream on cable with buzzy dramas such as *The*

51

Shield and *Mad Men*. And media economics tells us mass-interest titles that also inspire strong passion are like rainbow-striped unicorns. The feasibility of intentionally developing such titles is nearly impossible.

It is magical thinking to expect that a single title, or even a few titles, will warrant subscription from more than the 1 per cent of those deeply invested in television and film. Rather than expecting 'must watch' titles to drive subscribers, the commercial viability of a service depends on its value proposition and distinctiveness. Yes, a title – maybe a handful of titles – offers distinction, but more than that is required in the current competitive space. Several major services came to market in 2019 and 2020, and, even with a global pandemic driving viewing, not all will survive. The inevitable failures will not indicate that 'streaming is dead' or 'the end of streaming' – as the breathless headlines will suggest. But, more likely, these failures will result from services' lack of something distinctive enough to attract subscribers or to warrant an additional video subscription.

This is especially a risk among the owned-IP SVODs launching from Hollywood conglomerates. Consider the content strategy of these services: 'distribute titles we own' – titles that were developed for a range of broadcasters and cable channels or for theatrical release. Most have announced minimal bespoke strategies for their SVOD service. We'll have a *Friends* reunion show. *The Mandalorian*. A show with Jennifer Aniston. Having decades of well-known intellectual property at your disposal is much better than not having IP, but the IP isn't enough. It needs to be linked to a strategy, and the strategy needs to address all the ways the affordances of SVODs allow for and encourage content strategies different from those of linear ad-supported channels. This is especially crucial for those services that imagine they will offer a comparable value proposition to Netflix on a global scale. Most of the people who write about SVODs think about television and video for many hours a day. Most people who watch SVODs do not think about these things. They come home from long days at work; many perform a second shift of domestic work and then, if they are lucky, might have an hour or two of leisure to enjoy watching something they like. They do not want to think about what to watch, they do not want to figure out what is on what service, they simply want something to watch. Even enthusiastic viewers will be price sensitive enough that a service will need to provide consistent ongoing value to maintain subscription. The easiest thing to do is to watch the service(s) you already have. It is noticeable that, twenty years into this transition – in which SVODs offer more if not better programming and a better experience – most nightly viewership still involves linear channels. Yes, it is declining, but at a pace that makes clear that most people cannot be bothered to tolerate any level of friction in their experience of viewing.

There isn't a magic number of services most people will subscribe to or a single library strategy. This is all really Business 101. Find a hole in the marketplace big enough that your subscriber fees can cover your costs and fill it. But the value proposition is based on the service as the whole, not access to one title or a few. There may only be room for one global general service such as Netflix that aims to commission extensive bespoke content for subscribers as a 'global' audience (though Amazon and Apple may persist because they aren't really in the video business). Outside the US, there is likely room for nation-specific services that offer something different than Netflix. And there are specialty services that might be viable but won't scale. Specialty players aren't going to have the balance sheet totals of the multi-territory general SVODs, but they also don't have the same costs. In other words, goal number one is to be profitable, and you don't have to make the most money to succeed. We understand this in other media, but the bias towards the 'streaming war' frame can obscure this. For example, in interviewing Soumya Sriraman, the CEO of Britbox, *Variety*'s Andy Wallenstein was dismissive of its potential as a specialty service, assuming it must compete directly with giants such as Netflix. But just as *Variety* persists as a specialty publisher despite overall revenue that doesn't compare to that of the *New York Times*, both can succeed.

Related, the flexibility of subscribing to SVODs – at least in 2022 – is much greater than has been the case of multichannel service. Typically, if you 'had cable', it was a long and ongoing relationship. The SVOD services would love for that to be the model of adoption, but this is unlikely, except among subscribers who aren't price sensitive. The ability to start and stop subscriptions easily enables customers to transfer in and out of libraries. In the analogue days, you might choose to watch 'what's on' NBC on Thursday night, while, in 2022, you might choose to watch Disney+ in May. If the value proposition is good, you'll stick with it for June, or longer – which is what the services are hoping for. But it isn't likely that subscribers will maintain more than the subscriptions used in a given week or month on an ongoing basis. This is a really different way of thinking than was the case of past distribution technologies. The challenge for the services is first to provide enough value to compel viewers to try, and then stay beyond a month, or at least come back once a year.

3

Subscriber Funding: On Success Metrics, Programme Strategies, and Demographics

SVODs use different metrics to evaluate success than those used by linear television. Any linear television executive will tell you the defining experience of their job was receiving the overnight ratings report every morning. But knowing how many of an SVOD's subscribers watched any particular show, especially in the first hours of its availability, is far less important. Rather, the most crucial metric for SVODs is monthly change in the number of subscribers.

After decades of the norms of linear television, it is disorienting to process the idea that the number of people who watch *Stranger Things* on Netflix on a particular night or watched *Soul* the day Disney+ released it isn't vitally important to these services. We are so accustomed to these norms that a cottage industry of analysts blogs obsessively about any hint of high viewing of a title, or about the market-by-market Top 10 lists Netflix now releases daily, as if such measures were still the gold standard of evaluation. Of course SVODs are deeply concerned about how many people watch a title in evaluating the wisdom of their licensing and commissions. And, yes, these services use number of viewers as *a* metric for evaluating the return on investment of their licensing or commissioning fees. But SVODs are not in the business of assembling giant audiences. They are in the business of attracting and retaining subscribers. And the number of accounts viewing a title isn't nearly as important as in the linear ad-supported sector – or, for that matter, in terms of opening weekend box office.

There are two reasons the measure of success differs, both derived from the difference in business model. Most basically, SVOD revenue comes from subscribers rather than advertisers or from direct transaction – as in the case of paying to see a movie at a cinema. SVODs have to offer enough value to viewers to warrant payment – ideally, repeated monthly payment. The core business of linear ad-funded services is not to please viewers. Rather, it is to attract their attention so that it can be sold to advertisers. Linear ad-supported services sell the attention to specific commercials aired at specific times. The ratings for *Grey's Anatomy* aren't a measure of how 'good' a show it is but an indication of how good it is at attracting attention at a particular time, and its rating is important because it tells us how many might have watched the commercials in it. Executives evaluate a show's ratings against the other options 'on' at the same time.

The contribution of each title to producing revenue is far clearer in this business model; it is a relentless game of attracting and selling attention. Viewers who record shows and watch them later or skip through commercials diminish attention that can be sold. The crucial indicator is the scale of audience for each commercial aired, and each programme can be evaluated for its capability to attract attention.[1] But where linear ad-supported services face a daily report card, those for SVODs come with monthly subscriber accounting. It is difficult to ascribe an accurate valuation of the role any title plays in that performance because it is not simply a question of how many people watched, but also to what extent watching provided value that encouraged continued subscription.

In ad-supported viewing or theatrical exhibition, the number of people watching a title ties directly to success. Subscriptions to bundles are different. Success of the service derives from number of paying subscribers, so the service develops metrics that indicate subscriber satisfaction. Titles that deliver a lot of viewers are valuable, but they aren't the only way titles can be valuable. When you are selling discrete goods – the audience available at 8:30 on Sunday evening or seats to the evening showing of *Star Wars* – the number of people is a direct measure of the success of the title. But Netflix derives no more benefit from 100,000 Canadians all watching *Tiger King* on a Tuesday than if those 100,000 viewers were spread across 1,000 different shows and all far from approaching most-watched status.

SVODs don't need viewers to watch at a particular time, nor do they need audiences to watch en masse. SVODs are not more successful if most people watch a particular title than if the same number of people spread their viewing over tens or hundreds of titles (although there are cost benefits if they can provide the same subscriber value with less content). This is the second reason their measure of success differs: SVODs offer a bundle of titles in the form of access to a library. Any title is just part of the value that compels viewer subscription. Certainly, too few titles of interest in that bundle risks churn (cancelling the service). But, in practice, the point at which value drops too low depends a lot on bundle price and subscriber price sensitivity.

Video 'bundles' have a bad reputation in the US because of the legacy of cable packages and a perception among viewers that bundling leads to high prices. What happened in US cable was not about the inefficiency of bundles but caused by a series of anti-competitive markets that were allowed to prevent market forces from operating.[2] Bundles are actually a pretty efficient way to support a diverse array of programming, especially in a model of pure subscriber funding.[3]

Bundling also explains how SVODs can pursue programming strategies different from linear broadcasters. The on-demand technology allows them to bundle viewers around different titles and even entirely different content types. This too is very different from linear strategies aimed at amassing attention for a single title, hour by hour. Not only does the revenue model deprioritize mass audience building, but the distribution technology enables it to use a diversified bundle of content to simultaneously serve viewers with wide-ranging tastes and interests.

Selling access to a bundle – typically a month at a time, though there is nothing natural about this 'norm' – makes how many subscribers watch on a particular day, let alone view a specific title, an insubstantial indicator. It is one data point of many. Viewers might not watch anything on a SVOD most of a month but derive enough value to keep paying just because it offered a marathon of viewing one rainy weekend. I often do the maths of comparing a month's fee to what it would cost for one family outing to the movies – how much value will we get from a month of Disney+? We still take those outings (we were never regular cinema goers), but the comparative value of SVODs – even if we aren't watching much – is strong.

Of course SVODs monitor daily viewing and likely have many measures that have validity as proxies of satisfaction. Certainly hours of use, perhaps per viewer, is an indication of value. But the hegemony of linear norms probably leads us to overvalue 'quantity' metrics. As explored later, many SVODs offer content distinct from what viewers can get from linear ad-funded services. That distinction is a qualitative measure related to sensibility or passion for particular content. To phrase this mathematically, the value of being able to access that distinct content operates as a coefficient that moderates the value of the time being spent. For example, imagine you could rank all content on a scale from one to ten in terms of its value to you. One hour of content that ranks a ten provides more satisfaction than nine hours of content rating a one. SVODs have no certain indication of each subscriber's content valuation, so they don't know whether the quantity of viewing represents high or low value. But they can correlate library viewing over time and in relation to levels of subscriber churn.

It is worth remembering that it was often clear that number of viewers alone did not guide HBO content decisions (a legacy subscriber service), and that HBO has also only released viewer data selectively. Subscriber-funded services are concerned most with number of subscribers, new subscribers, and cancellation. SVODs are able to know much more about the viewing behaviour of each account making those choices and consequently are not fixated on the number of people viewing any particular title – or at a particular time – in the way those data points are of crucial significance to an ad-supported channel. The ability to focus content strategy on developing a bundle of content that generally provides value – albeit in different ways to different viewers – leads SVODs to prioritize different content than that best suited to the conditions of linear ad-supported services. The next section of this chapter explores the implications of subscriber funding on programme strategy and addresses how the industrial features of SVODs compel content different from linear ad-funded services and how the primary metric of subscriber level may encourage the commissioning and licensing of content unlikely to be widely popular.

To state the obvious, then, the performance of any single title is of less clear value to an SVOD than to a linear ad-supported service. Both services have two stages of evaluation. The foremost measure for ad-funded services is the attention generated by particular shows, while for SVODs it is monthly subscriber levels. Second to these are measures that indicate how efficiently they achieve those metrics. Both use video to achieve their primary goal, so this secondary measure addresses the different priorities each employs in evaluating how their content contributes to that primary goal.

For linear ad-supported services, this is fairly straightforward. The number of viewers attracted by a programme correlates precisely to the revenue it contributes. There are some other factors. Advertisers value the attention of viewers based on various characteristics: a show that attracts fewer overall viewers but high levels of particularly advertiser-valued viewers may yield higher prices. Also the costs of programmes differ: a lower cost show that delivers the same level and quality of attention is more efficient than a more expensive show. And there are various reputational factors that matter. It can be valuable for an ad-supported service to have some shows that attract award nominations and critical praise, because this can help ensure talent seeks to work with it and provides promotion that might encourage more viewers.

For SVODs, evaluating the value of individual titles to the bundle is far more complicated. Did all the buzz and significant viewing of *Tiger King* in 2020 really lead to more subscribers or to some not cancelling Netflix? Titles that attract buzz are valuable to these services as unpaid marketing, especially for newer services. Each feature article or discussion of the series on social media gets the name of the service in front of people and promotes subscription. Similarly, pursuit of industry awards such as Oscars and Emmys bestows unpaid marketing and positive promotion of the value of the service. Having a non-subscriber think 'I'd like to watch that show' is the most valuable promotion available to SVODs.

Beyond the need to conceptualize SVODs differently from services supported by advertising, this difference in metrics creates practical challenges. Advertiser-funded media feature very clear metrics of commercial success: gather the most attention among advertiser-desired groups. Such metrics are easily assessed, have long been part of public discourse, and are reasonably available to researchers or to journalists writing about the role of these services in culture or the economy. Subscriber-funded services develop far more complicated metrics of commercial success that are typically closely held, especially in the case of SVODs. Certainly, inferences can be made based on services' decisions to commission or end series, but it is difficult to develop the depth of strategic understandings that we possess for ad-supported services without more publicly available consumption data. And it is crucial to be on guard for the hegemony of linear norms to creep into thinking when bits of data do appear.

Content worth paying for

It follows that different metrics of success warrant different programming strategies. So how do SVODs' pursuit of subscribers lead them to commission or license different content?

This is difficult to discuss generally, because, as the second part of the book explores, the SVODs are not unified in strategy because of the different combinations of structuring characteristics. But it can generally be argued that the strategies used by linear ad-supported channels to attract the most attention at a given moment are not the same strategies that compel people to pay for a service. Subscriber funding arguably changes almost everything about a video service's priorities from those with which we are familiar. It changes the metrics of evaluation and the strategies used to achieve those metrics.

On some level this is obvious – who would pay for something they can get for free? Yes, the experience offered by SVODs is enough to compel some to payment, but there is also a strong sense of a need for content 'worth' paying for. SVODs add to their value proposition when they offer content viewers can't get elsewhere, but that can be many things.

As media economists Bruce Owen and Steven Wildman explain it, the most mass hits are often less satisfying to consumers than those programmes that are able to service more specific tastes.[4] This encourages content with different characteristics for SVODs than that deemed most desirable to linear ad-supported services.

The on-demand delivery of SVODs allows them to prioritize more individualized tastes without concern about simultaneously not serving other tastes. Surprisingly little has been written about subscriber funding and its implications for strategy, though I suppose it is not really surprising given how uncommon pure subscriber funding was across media industries until SVODs. (To be clear, the inclusion of advertising on most of what is termed 'pay-TV' makes these channels primarily subject to the strategies of ad-funding and audience aggregation.)

As of 2022, it is difficult to speak generally of how SVODs illustrate different programme strategies. Chapter 8 explores Netflix's strategy, but it is distinct from that of the other general, multinational-to-global services that mostly rely on owned IP, much of which was originally developed for linear ad-supported services or theatrical distribution. But it is crucial to recognize that there is good reason to expect different programme strategies and that SVODs will measure the success of these programmes in ways different than has been the case for linear television or theatrical box office.

Just as with linear ad-supported television, viewers are frustrated when SVODs cease production of their favourite shows. Or we wonder how what seems a comparatively brilliant show could have only two or three seasons when others more mediocre go on and on. The conditions of commercial linear ad-supported television led the industry to equate more episodes with 'better' shows, but all those episodes resulted because the economics of that system rewards longevity. An underlying belief that 'more is better' persists, and this is not the case.

Of course everyone wants more of their favourite thing, but SVODs don't prioritize long-running series in the same manner because of the difference of their business. The linear ad-supported norms of success – in the US at least – reward content that generates the largest mass audience in prime time. In addition to earning advertiser dollars for the networks that pay their first license fee, these titles developed a number of episodes and a commercial track record that allowed them to be sold most extensively into US secondary markets (local affiliates, cable channels) and internationally. Such buyers sought series with many episodes, which led to seasons of twenty-two episodes and the goal of a long-running series; for a long time, the standard necessary was five seasons to amass a hundred episodes.[5]

Twenty years ago, critics castigated these norms. For the tedium they created. For the many series that outlived their creativity but continued production because that's what the system incentivised. For how the system kept making more episodes simply because there was more money to make, not more stories to be told. Thoughtful analysts recognized the industrial constraints in the system: how the long-running series was valuable because it limited the marketing spend required; how it delivered stability in the schedule that could be used to launch new shows; how such shows often provided a training ground for the next generation of creatives; and how, in turn, it made the range of stories and series likely to be produced very narrow.

The goal of attracting the attention of millions of people with the same series for hundreds of hours of television limits the range of stories likely to be told. It explains the abundance of franchise series about cops, docs, and lawyers and mundane comedies about families and friends. It explains the lack of miniseries. There are few opportunities for new shows if a title is commanding twenty-two hours in a schedule a year and producing more than five seasons of episodes. In short, these norms explain a lot about why US television long offered such a narrow range of content.

The hegemony of linear norms leads us to believe that series with more episodes are 'better', but this is the wrong priority. Series should have the number of episodes a story needs, and a system that allows for a greater diversity of stories and story lengths is better than a system that requires a single norm. In the linear ad-supported US system, more episodes typically meant more money for producers, so it became difficult to tell whether more stories needed to be told or the financial and reputational rewards drove additional seasons. A producer-centric approach to this question would argue that the number of episodes the lead creative wants to tell is the best number of episodes. Sometimes the entity funding production – as well as fans – want more, as is arguably the case of a show such as *Fleabag*. More often, the service wants fewer and stops paying, thus ending the story.

When an SVOD caps a series at two seasons, it shouldn't be regarded as a failure for the service or the creative team. The industrial conditions don't reward long runs in the same way as in the linear ad-supported model. SVODs don't need a hundred episodes to sell the show in other markets; they aren't going to sell them. Instead, the internal calculus seeks to determine at what point additional episodes fail to add more value to the library than warranted by the cost of producing them. As with many of the contrasts between linear ad-supported television and SVOD commissions, it isn't that one mode of production is necessarily better than the other, just that the differences in these models produce different constraints and opportunities. Of course it is still disappointing when favourite shows end after a season or two, but we shouldn't assume the 'natural' condition of series must be five or more seasons or that anything less than this reflects negatively.

A greater range of stories are being told because the revenue model and distribution technology of SVODs can make them commercially viable. But the economics of this system cannot support hundreds of episodes of all those stories, nor do many of their creative concepts warrant more episodes. Sometimes long-running series produced great episodes late in their runs or were able to depict character evolutions as a result of having many seasons. Notably, there is nothing preventing long-running series on SVODs. I suspect if a series generated a notable level of interest, we'd see more than the typical two or three seasons. But broad hits are also not the only content strategy available for these services, as the investigation of Netflix's content strategy explores in Part II. The changes to video industries have made them businesses of singles and doubles – to use baseball terms. There are both advantages and consequences for creativity, money-making, and storytelling in this, but there is more flexibility than amid the linear ad-supported hegemony.

We are still in the process of building an understanding of these SVOD constraints and of what constitutes success and failure for SVODs. Various production norms developed as a result of the prioritization of making at least a hundred episodes. The system of success and talent reward in SVOD commissions is entirely different because the way series are valued and made valuable are entirely different. In the SVOD realm, individual titles aren't given market value because they aren't expected to be sold outside the service. They are fully financed by the service rather than deficit financed by the production company or financed through selling later/other distribution rights, and thus don't require additional sales to cover costs.

Once one industrial norm changes as dramatically as those introduced by SVODs, there is a domino chain of knock-on implications. The different practices of SVODs in commissioning and keeping series requires many adjustments throughout various business trans-actions, and the structure by which creative talent is paid is a big one. We'll get to that in the next chapter's exploration of the SVOD business model.

It would be an improvement if the industrial practices that are normalized in SVOD production incentivise producing just the number of episodes that a story needs. Creatives shouldn't feel they lose an opportunity by having fewer seasons than past benchmarks or that hundreds of episodes are better than ten. The old system of reward led us to believe hundreds of episodes are better. Hundreds of episodes made a very few people very rich, but those conditions also made it impossible to tell many of the stories that now exist.

Video without a demographic lens

In addition to the biases that result from the hegemony of linear thinking, the *hegemony of demographic thinking* is a set of habits and assumptions that tie to the ad-supported dominance of linear television, the priorities that resulted, and the extent of what could be known about the linear audience. Demographic thinking imagines the audience based on features such as gender, age groups, and income levels. It ties assumptions of preferences for different types of programming to these characteristics; for example, the idea that romantic comedies attract women or that a female lead character will attract more female viewers. This isn't necessarily wrong, but it isn't as right as marketing romantic comedies to people known to watch romantic comedies.

Demographic thinking leads us to misunderstand SVODs in two ways. The first has to do with the priorities of these services. An SVOD service doesn't care about the demographics of its subscribers, only that they are subscribers. Advertiser-funded services prioritize different audience demographics because, in general, advertisers will pay more to reach wealthier and younger people. Other characteristics can be important based on the product and the people most likely to buy it. Also, because audience scale is the primary metric in ad-funded television, demographic thinking is used to expand that viewership – for example, in a drama about a woman, add a brother character so that men might watch.

SVODs don't care about the demographics of who subscribes. Beyond an ability to pay, subscribers are equally valuable regardless of their demographic features. Indeed, SVODs have a monthly fee and, more significantly, require subscribers be able to afford the cost of and have access to internet service, so this narrows the market of available consumers to those who can afford such things. But an SVOD doesn't prefer wealthier to poor viewers in the way ad-supported television does.

Secondly, the use data available to SVODs allow them to sort their subscribers by far more sophisticated and relevant measures than demographic character-istics. To date, Netflix, with its pure-play corporate position and gradually developing bespoke IP, illustrates how different possible strategies can be. Instead of demographics, Netflix sorts by tastes identified based on viewing behaviour. A quick perusal of the Netflix library and its commissions makes certain targets clear. Various analysts have called these 'taste clusters' or 'taste communities.'[6] Instead of a demographic such as 'women over forty', Netflix programmes for people who like dark political thrillers, empowering romantic comedies, or cynical comedies about motherhood (mom-coms). (These are my taste communities; they'll keep reappearing because, when I look at Netflix, they are mostly what I see – which is a whole other issue. I know there are many other clusters; substitute what you see.) Where an ad-supported service tries to build an audience by imagining it as different demographic features to aggregate, Netflix imagines their subscribers and potential subscribers as defined by a variety of tastes that it services through an array of content types, tones, desired experiences, and sensibilities (more expla-nation in chapter 7).

Programming unbound from demographics enables a greater range of programmes and stories. I think back to my research about the series *Any Day Now* (Lifetime, late 1990s) and how Lifetime – then branded as 'Television for Women' – pressured the writers to tell more stories about the teen daughter instead of the forty-something protagonists. And I think about how my tastes do and don't map onto what might be imagined as the tastes of the forty-something woman. It is definitely the case that I find more on Netflix that 'speaks to me' than on broadcast television or at the movie theatre. This is partially the result of the fact that I seek programming more unconventional than conventional. When I view, I do so with focus, and I want something that demands that I pay attention and connect dots on my own. Such factors might alienate other viewers, thus poorly suiting these features to shows aimed at attracting the most viewers. These preferences have nothing to do with my gender, age, or income.

It is important to consider the intersection of SVODs' on-demand capability with all demographics being equally weighted. In trying to create mass appeal, linear programmers followed the hegemony of demographic thinking to overrepresent audiences more valuable to advertisers. This explains the absence of series featuring characters much over fifty or stories about life's later years, as well as many others. Netflix can develop programmes about older characters that might attract younger viewers as well, but its on-demand delivery makes it unlikely to be narrowly identified with any one type of programming.

Of course demographics often do map onto tastes, frankly in ways I'm not sure we understand. I don't want to throw decades of scholarship about representation and identity out of the window, but it also seems that Netflix has been able to identify tastes and approach casting and other creative inclusion in a way that develops programming that addresses diversity in a manner not driven by demographic thinking. This

71

is an idea that needs more evidence to investigate satisfactorily.

The twin impacts of operating outside the hegemony of linear norms and of demographic thinking explain why SVODs can be expected to deviate from linear ad-supported television. Not radically so: many are still negotiating the strategy needed to be a mass-market product, or at least in a majority of homes. But I think of it as shifting content norms 45 degrees to the left – not enough to be profoundly distinct, but askew enough for differentiation. This differentiation is needed to entice people to pay for the service and is made possible because the services can offer content to many different tastes at once. It is also made possible by the depth of intelligence they collect about what different viewers actually watch – not imagined differences between men and women or young and old, but apparent patterns of behaviour tied to different titles with identifiable content features. To date, only Netflix offers evidence of understanding its business as a matter of conglomerating niches and of a strategy focused on differentiation. As newer services are in market longer and evidence either long-term stability and strong subscriber numbers or steady pivots in the face of failed expectations, we'll learn more about the strategies of this sector.

4

Licensing, Labour, Regulation, and Recommendation

Most of the distinction of SVODs ties to the major structuring factors of subscriber funding, on-demand delivery, and – for several – multi-territory reach. There are also more micro-business strategies that are quite distinct from the norms of video production for linear ad-supported television or the typical tiered release structure of Hollywood films. It is worth drawing out some of these particular practices, such as the underlying payment structures used in licensing content and how viewers pay to access them, because these also contribute to SVODs' different strategies and priorities. Notably, there has been little variation among the practices used, but, despite this largely singular approach, there is nothing 'natural' or inherent to the common practices of SVODs.

A key difference can be seen in the terms for commissioning content. Netflix has done the most commissioning to date, but its practices are being adopted by other SVODs in their bespoke commissions. Compared to previous norms of linear ad-funded services, SVODs license programs for a *long period of time* – typically years, or many years in the case of commissions. When an SVOD commissions or licenses content, it pays a *flat fee* that is not tied to how many times a programme is watched.[1] And, somewhat related, it is worth acknowledging that *users pay a flat monthly fee* for access regardless of the amount of programming viewed. These three features of SVODs' business model establish the financial foundation of their content strategies. Other services might offer video but, if they pay for content based on how many times a title is viewed, pay no licence (because they own it) or offer different tiers of service based on how much is viewed, then analysis needs to account for how such practices will drive different strategies. Notably, there are many different practices that a subscriber-funded, on-demand service could use.

The COVID-19 pandemic made apparent some of the implications of these dynamics. Even though viewing of SVODs increased given the additional in-home time many had available, this surge changed little for the services outside of those that had strong subscriber growth. The SVODs gained no financial benefit from people watching more hours – which could be the case if the underlying business model were different. Fortunately for the services, the fees needed to pay for shows – for those that license content – also didn't change just because many likely tallied an increase in views. And, fortunately for viewers, the fee they paid for their SVODs did not increase even though their use of the service may have doubled or more.

To be clear, there is no reason that these should be norms. Other payment structures are possible – such as payment based on use. Imagine, in contrast, a video service comparable to Spotify – a bundle subscription fee with truly vast access. What if a single service had 'all' the video and paid licence holders based on what is viewed? How much would you pay a month for such a service? Such a model probably couldn't support commissioning new content but would be a far more viewer-friendly way to access older titles. Could such a service drive more viewing than the ability to buy specific titles in the Apple, Amazon, or Google Play libraries? It's an interesting thought experiment, even if unlikely ever to happen. The point is that different financial terms would change programming strategies significantly. Drawing attention to how the current practice works also helps explain the distinctive content and subscriber retention strategies SVODs use.

Producing for SVODs

All of the underlying industrial characteristics that differentiate SVODs from other video distributors have consequences for other aspects of their norms. Because audiences can access particular titles over periods of years, SVODs aim to keep their commissions in their library for perpetuity. This requires a different structure for remunerating those who make that content than has been the norm for content created initially for linear ad-funded services. How content is financially valued and how the talent that creates it is paid also profoundly distinguish SVODs from many pre-digital video norms.

Changing a component of industrial norms is rather similar to Newton's Third Law of Motion – it might not bring an equal and opposite reaction, but changing the terms by which a distributor purchases content or how users pay results in corresponding consequences. These changes are what allow the differences in programme strategies described above, but the forces that adjust commercial boundaries also require adjustments in how people who make the content are paid.

When Netflix started as another licensing window – and thus consistent with the established ecosystem of programme licensing – the questions of how to pay talent when distributing video via the internet were problems the rights' holders had to sort out. But once Netflix began commissioning content with the aim of monetizing those titles in ways different from linear norms of windowed resale, adjustments were needed in remuneration models that are based on selling content again and again.

An SVOD isn't just another content commissioner – it is a subscriber-funded content commissioner. Because the primary aim is not to attract the most people to watch a title at a specific time but to entice more people to subscribe to the service, it makes sense for SVODs to keep commissions exclusive to the service for perpetuity. This is not at all similar to how video distribution has worked (HBO and other purely subscriber-funded services excepted). But this contrast, of keeping content available on the service rather than allowing for its sale in different places and to different kinds of distribution services, requires very distinct terms in how it pays creators.

Particular titles don't make money on SVODs – or they don't derive a computable market value comparable to summing the licence fees paid for a title in different markets. The hegemony of linear norms leads us to assume SVOD titles gain capital within the service by attracting viewers, but SVODs have different expectations of and aims for different titles. Where linear ad-supported television simply prioritizes titles that attract the most attention, the content most valuable to an SVOD is not necessarily the content most watched. An SVOD can compute a return of investment based on the number of views, which it perhaps multiplies by some coefficient that attempts to factor in the perceived value of that content for different subscribers, but that is not a comparable calculation to the tally of licence fees paid in the open market for rights to a title.

This may not be *Stranger Things*' 'the upside down', but it is certainly sideways from how video distribution has worked and illustrates why evaluations of SVODs' remuneration structure should not be compared to those of linear ad-supported services or other window-based contexts. The equity and fairness of SVODs' creative payment can – and should – be evaluated, but that assessment cannot be based on what is 'normal' in other industrial contexts. It is too soon to know in what ways the terms of those payments are better or worse for creatives; the new norms are still very much in development. It also may never be possible to assess because the situation of creative talent at different levels varies so greatly. It is unlikely that the incomprehensible money earned by the fewer than 1 per cent who have profit participation in shows such as *Law & Order* and *Friends* will be possible in this system. That is a consequence of the lack of mass hits as well the different economics. A mass hit doesn't equal a big pay day for a subscriber-funded service or those making content for it.

Massive overhaul in remuneration is warranted. The analogue-era system of residual payment was developed to ensure additional payments to certain creative talent when titles continued to earn revenue after the first distribution window. Titles in SVOD libraries likewise continue to have value, but it is difficult to determine that financial value. Specific titles do not have profits, and the old metric of 'more viewers equal greater success' isn't as central to the SVOD model. As a result, the norm emerging for SVODs means talent is paid an upfront fee for service. There are indirect benefits that can be accrued by talent for success within the SVODs' measures. For example, success begets the next deal and a better negotiating position. Those regarded as exceptional are earning special deals, as creators such as Shonda Rhimes, Ryan Murphy, and Kenya Barris have achieved at Netflix, which also has offered subsequent deals to talent in other countries. Base pay structures need to acknowledge a single payment for work and be adjusted upwards in some cases. If contracts are becoming less bespoke and defaulting to simple base pay rates, then maybe talent agents add less to this process and are less necessary or warrant a lower share of earnings. Again, make one change and other changes follow on.

Creators, of course, will make comparisons between the terms of producing for broadcast versus SVOD – at least those in the privileged position to be choosing between opportunities at different kinds of services. Many long-standing factors weigh on those decisions, and US creatives have been making this calculation for two decades in pursuing cable commissions that allow a broader creative canvas but typically accrue lower earnings. As Harvard economist Richard Caves argues, creative industries are peculiar in the way some economic givens do not operate; talent can be motivated by 'art for art's sake' and derive value from factors such as the ability to tell a specific story or to do so in a specific way, even if it means lower earnings than for another project, for which they have less passion but which is more lucrative.[2] The residual revenue in linear ad-supported norms is also highly uncertain; it is difficult to predict what titles will have a long life through windows and those that won't. Those with profit participation have a chance at windfall, but often those chances turn out to be as valuable as a losing lottery ticket.

Instead of perceiving SVODs' different remuneration terms as a problem, it is also important to acknowledge that it is forcing change on what were already broken remuneration structures – at least in the US, where conglomeration had brought crises related to self-dealing. The conditions that enabled conglomerates to own the titles produced in their studios and use them across a range of channels have produced many concerns about equity to talent with various residual and profit participation rights. There is also a trade-off between profit and creative opportunity. The conditions of creating for mass audiences made substantial earnings possible, but they also allowed only a narrow range of storytelling.

Creating for SVODs compares more precisely to contexts different than those assumed (movie and television). A SVOD commission may be most like freelance journalism. That commission contributes to the value of a larger, bundled good (the library) and tends not to accrue earnings beyond that bundle. SVODs offer creatives different terms than do linear services because their business is different. The reason for the difference needs to be appreciated because it is impossible to change so many other aspects of the business without changing remuneration norms as well.

Regulating SVODs

The framing of SVODs as functionally 'like' linear ad-supported services with long histories of regulation and supports in many countries leads to confused and inefficient approaches to incorporating them into regulatory frameworks that govern other video providers. A key problem has been the assumption that SVODs are most comparable to linear ad-supported channels when they are more similar to video rental stores.

The video rental store is a more commensurable precursor to SVODs than linear ad-supported channels in many ways. This should have been quite obvious to me as an American familiar with Netflix 1.0, but it took a while to sort out. In many places where Netflix never delivered movies by mail, Netflix and SVOD services became perceived as more commensurate to television, probably because the SVODs allow content to flow into a home without a physical form and have relied significantly on series, whereas 'video rental' tends more to conjure up movies. However, many aspects of the SVOD business model render it more similar to video rental than to television.

The key way this framing is important is in terms of how SVODs are considered for cultural policy regulation or taxation. European cultural policy-makers moved quickly to enact local content quotas comparable to those faced by linear channels on the titles offered in libraries. In contrast, in most countries, video rental stores were not subject to the kinds of local content quotas expected of television broadcasters, and for good reason. Video rental stores couldn't *decide the schedule* of movies that appeared in your house, often amid a fairly *narrow range of options* – two of broadcasting's more notable powers that are not available to video rental or SVODs. Further, video-cassette rental didn't use public resources such as spectrum or require the public infrastructure of cable and satellite deployment, which some countries also used as justification for requiring public service from these providers.[3]

Video stores also didn't sell the attention of viewers to advertisers and thus did not aim to assemble mass audiences. Rather, like the SVODs, in order to succeed they needed to be accountable to the tastes of people who paid to rent movies. Of course they had the ability to make some things available and others not, but if their choices were out of line with the marketplace they'd soon be out of business. This might mean a video store would endeavour to provide great differentiation if that's what suited its neighbourhood or clientele or offer deep stocks of blockbuster hits where the tastes ran to the mainstream. Video stores had limited capacity and could certainly narrow the range of options available, but their curatorial impact was minimal in comparison to the circulation power of broadcasters. And, as a result, it was left to the marketplace to regulate the mix of content they offered.

Following this comparison, there are good reasons to approach regulating SVODs more like video rental stores than broadcasters. First, revenue model. People pay for the service, and they pay only if it provides a value proposition (content × experience) that they desire. The business of video stores depended on delivering desired titles. People patronized video stores based on their convenience and the likelihood they would offer desired content. This is quite different from what broadcasters do in trying to attract the attention of the most viewers by constructing an audience. Moreover, video stores transacted with individuals; they could service the tastes of different customers with different titles rather than forcing them to a common title.

The basis of broadcast regulation varies by country, but in many places the rules applied to commercial broadcasters derive from the limited available spectrum they use to transmit signals and an underlying understanding of that spectrum as warranting some service to the public because the spectrum is a national good. Spectrum used for broadcasting is rarely owned by broadcasters; rather, they are afforded the ability to use it to construct audiences – which they often sell to advertisers – and are expected to perform some basic levels of public service, or pay a fee, in exchange for its use. The basis of government regulation of the internet also varies by country, but it is difficult to mount the same arguments of scarcity that apply to broadcasting; nor is video access the sole purpose of broadband infrastructure. Other features of the technology also warrant different regulatory consideration. Broadcast signals come to a television whether you want them or not. This inability to block signals is the basis of a lot of US content requirements.

The question of whether regulatory frames from broadcasting are outmoded given the modern video distribution ecosystem is a separate question from whether or how to regulate SVODs. Modernization of policies is needed in many places – modernization that acknowledges the complexity of twenty-first-century communication technologies and responds appropriately instead of applying solutions developed for analogue technologies, markets of scarcity, and 'free' service. Twenty-first-century communication technologies pose direct and indirect challenges to the previous regulatory equilibrium. The distinctive features of these technologies warrant not only revisiting the primary aims and goals of policies for other video distribution technologies but also considering how modern technologies provide new tools for achieving policy aims. Some things once central to audiovisual policy have become lesser concerns in the current environment, while new, quite urgent issues stand in their place.

To that context, I assert SVODs are more like video rental stores than broadcasters. They construct libraries rather than schedules, and, as a result, content quotas are a particularly ill-suited policy mechanism. Their complementarity to existing services requires a distinct approach that acknowledges their disparate affordances and goals. Metaphors of 'levelling the playing field' by treating broadcasters and SVODs the same way are poorly considered. Is the playing field of train and plane travel level? Could it ever be? No, because, even though both provide transportation, their affordances differ. Likewise there are different types of video distribution technology that require approaches attuned to their distinctions.

This isn't to say SVODs can't or shouldn't be regulated. Underlying policy goals can be applied in ways that make sense given their incommensurable affordances and the corresponding complexity of the ecosystem this produces. Any effort that fails to appreciate the distinct affordances of SVODs is doomed to fail in delivering the intended policy aim or will do so in a way that produces unnecessary negative consequences for viewers, producers, and others.

In Australia, by way of example, a key debate is whether commercial broadcasters should continue to be mandated to produce local drama and children's programming, and whether such a quota system should also apply to SVODs. The latter is clearly a losing proposition (quotas on libraries are easy to manipulate, and this disregards the significant incommensurability between items in a library versus those in a schedule). Eliminating the rules on commercial broadcasters risks forms of Australian content unlikely to deliver large audiences – such as children's and drama programming – disappearing from commercial broadcasters entirely, although adapting the mandate and increasing funding support of the public broadcasters provides an alternative. Although Netflix shows a commitment to some multinational commissioning, it is doubtful that the service can be sustainable while delivering libraries of local drama characteristic of advertiser and public-funded channels in the scores of countries that it serves, and local content does not appear integrated into the strategy of many other multi-territory and global SVODs. That Netflix could match or replace the series commissioning of Australian broadcasters is simply an unreasonable expectation, but that doesn't mean it can't be part of a solution. There can't be a level playing field among such disparate entities, but there can be policies aimed at symbiosis that take account of the core structural differences among services. However, the starting point isn't merely applying the old tools to new services but rethinking the aims and priorities of cultural policies given the new ecosystem dynamics.

Recommendation on SVODs

Although issues related to recommendations, interfaces, and algorithms are crucial factors for some *internet-distributed services, the use of recommendations within a subscriber-funded sector is something wholly different than among ad-supported services.* SVODs are different from Facebook, other social media, and Google because revenue isn't directly tied to what viewers do with those recommendations. The business model of SVODs aligns search and algorithms to the user without regard for another party (an advertiser or, in the case of Amazon or Google, its own product). In these other cases reliant on selling attention, recommendations and how they are derived are first-order considerations. This isn't to suggest the AI behind the processes SVODs use to recommend content doesn't matter. Of course, no recommendation is neutral (just as no scheduling is), and recommendation is a vector of circulation power,[4] but the incentive for intentional manipulation to achieve an end contrary to aiding the user is reduced from contexts involving advertising. Subscriber funding means the goals of SVODs are aligned to viewer satisfaction, not advertiser satisfaction or other paid promotion. Moreover, since SVODs don't remunerate based on the number of times a title is viewed – the Spotify model – the incentive to manipulate recommendations is further diminished.

I've heard many express a belief that Netflix prioritizes its commissioned series in its algorithmic search results and library interface – and this dates to when commissions were a small part of the service. Maybe, but Netflix has little reason to put a heavy thumb on the scale in recommending commissioned content. Its business model doesn't lead it to derive substantively more value from my watching one title or another. Everything in its business model is aligned to encourage it to lead me to content that I've given it reason to believe I would like. If SVODs paid for content based on what people watch, its incentive to manipulate recommendation would be much stronger. I can't say whether it is or isn't the case that the algorithm prioritizes commissioned series. I suspect there is light encouragement of these titles. Netflix commissions are wholly unfamiliar to viewers, and their exclusivity is key to its distinctive value proposition, so, yes, it is beneficial to the service for subscribers to be aware of commissions and regard them as adding value. But there is no direct economic benefit in driving people to this content in the same way as if different financial practices supported the service – for example, when an Amazon search leads you to Amazon products or the incentive Facebook and YouTube have to serve me content that keeps me using their app longer so I can see more ads.

It is important to note that the recommendation capabilities are a key part of what makes the SVOD experience work – even if you swear the recommendations are always wrong. At a minimum, the ability to search content efficiently by title and genre and to have titles 'like this' recommended makes the conglomerated niche strategy viable. This is made very obvious if you use a service that has a decent sized library yet doesn't recommend and has 'dumber' search functionality.

The ability to target different programmes to different viewers is critical to the success of SVODs because access to content of interest is central to the value proposition that leads people to pay the monthly fee. As Netflix began releasing its first commissions, I was surprised that I didn't see the Adam Sandler films that had received a lot of press attention recommended to me. But then I found an interview with Netflix's Ted Sarandos explaining that the worst thing that could happen was for Netflix to recommend content contrary to a subscriber's sensibility, as this would feed negative word of mouth.[5] I had been thinking in linear norms – where opportunities of mass promotion such as the Super Bowl or major sporting events were particularly valuable because they allowed promotion of content to the widest possible audience. Netflix didn't blanket subscribers' home pages with Adam Sandler movies; only those who had a pattern of viewing that suggested they might like the movies were targeted.

Recommendation can be effective because SVODs can track past viewing. In other words, recommendations rely on data, which is a larger factor distinguishing SVODs than recommendations. At the risk of stating the obvious, data of actual viewing behaviour is an enormous game changer. It is the secret sauce; it explains how Netflix was able to overcome the hegemony of linear and demographic thinking to understand things about how and what people watch that remain largely known only to it. There has never been a way to know a lot about behaviour or sensibilities to efficiently and systematically investigate how people watch, and from which to make inferences about why they do so. Access to that data should reveal a lot that has been impossible to know because in the past data has been tied to discrete viewing acts.

SVODs also know how viewers actually use recommendations while those of us outside largely speculate. There are a lot of different features of recommendation, and I suspect there are patterns of behaviour characteristic of individuals, or perhaps most people exhibit different practices at different times. In theory, recommendations aid discovery of older titles, yet there is clearly a skew to the recent in the daily Top 10 titles data Netflix now shares. (Though just because the Top 10 titles are recently added doesn't tell us much about what else is happening among viewers, especially since we have no idea how much of the daily viewing the Top 10 shows account for.)

This issue of the introduction of unprecedented data is being felt across media industries, as when Spotify comes to know how many times different tracks are played and journalists learn just how many people click on their stories and stay long enough to read; media industries increasingly use that data to make judgements about preferences and to develop strategies and content in response. This data and how it can be used varies based on media goods and underlying revenue models. SVODs use this data differently than a company trying to monetize clicks. The days of the excuse 'nobody knows' that has been used in television and film to explain unexpected hits and failures are numbered.

5
Scale and Specialization

SVODs needn't be multi-territory, but several are, and this characteristic also distinguishes them from most linear ad-supported services. The multi-territory reach of these services is not wholly unprecedented. The transformation of primarily national to increasingly transnational dynamics began in earnest in the 1990s with the gradual launch of satellite channels in multiple countries, although programme trade began decades earlier.

Multi-territory SVODs have unprecedented scale. Indeed, channels such as Nickelodeon or MTV may have been available to as many homes around the globe as can now access SVODs, but their businesses were localized by territory in key ways. In order to find a place on cable or satellites services, these channels dealt with national-level policy-makers and service providers. Both these factors of national rules and national distributors required the channels to be somewhat nationally specific – although perhaps no more so than SVODs' use of nationally specific libraries. But, even more significantly, these channels operated in national advertising markets. Thus, even though a channel's brand may have had multi-territory reach, in programming the channel, executives were focused on attracting the attention of a significant enough audience *within a country* to sell to advertisers. In contrast, the multi-territory and global SVODs are able to imagine audiences without these national boundaries, which enables targeting of more particular tastes that transcend geographic borders.

Many of the multi-territory SVODs are not nearly as nationally specific as multi-territory cable channels. They do not have to craft deals with national telecom providers, although they are increasingly facing a patchwork of national regulations and taxation schemes that may result in bespoke libraries and territory specificity. But these are small nationalizing forces in comparison with how their business model and focus on subscriber funding alters the calculus of meeting audience needs. Global SVODs are unconcerned with trying to amass a sizable level of national attention around particular content. Instead, the multi-territory subscriber base allows such SVODs to cater to tastes and interests that might not be substantial enough to function as a viable market at the national scale or relative to the metrics of ad-funded services.

It remains fairly early days for multinational strategy, and, at this point, most services pursue a simple export strategy that imagines a multi-territory or global consumer with little national specificity. Although many national policy-makers have regarded this as a threat, it might also be an opportunity. Services with global scale have not been part of the television ecosystem. The combination of the strategies that derive from subscriber funding (needing to provide something of value) and multi-territory scale makes commercially viable tastes and sensibilities that were too small when segmented by nation. Part of the panic regarding the multi-territory and global services – a panic that reanimates old, largely discredited ideas of cultural imperialism – derives from hegemonies formed from the scarcity of linear ad-supported television and fails to recognize that subscribers actively choose these services and that services fail if they do not offer viewers a value proposition that compels payment. Concern also likely derives from the early prevalence of this multi-territory approach among those with the most capital and the consistency of a strategy based heavily on Hollywood content. However, as the sector matures, territory-specific SVODs also identify value propositions distinct from those seeking multi-territory or global scale.

A good example of how aggregating a multi-territory audience may allow content developed for groups too small to be serviced by linear ad-supported services is in the range of pre-teen and teen content being developed by multi-territory and global SVODs. The content desired by this age group is very specific; it tends to be inappropriate for younger children and of little interest to adults. In a context of valuing the most attention, linear ad-supported channels tried to push audience age boundaries and make content likely to appeal to teens and young adults, and perhaps assumed this was satisfactory for pre-teens as well (see commissions by US channels MTV, the CW, Freeform). However, SVODs can develop particular programmes for pre-teens and offer them globally in a way that amasses a significant enough audience to make them commercially viable (by adding value to family subscriptions). Where 'teen' drama was once a general category for linear ad-supported television and film, the SVOD commissions increasingly indicate significant subgenres within pre-teen and teen segments.

Importantly, sizable strategy differences exist even among those seeking global scale. The owned-IP services are still fairly new in the market and have yet to offer much evidence of pivoting from a traditional Hollywood strategy of designing vaguely American content for distribution around the world. The 'global' aspect of these services involves establishing direct-to-consumer relationships that eliminate the role of foreign channels that have redistributed Hollywood studios' content in decades past. In terms of competition, these services most threaten those linear channels that have relied on US content to attract attention. These SVODs largely reproduce content options already in the marketplace but offer much greater convenience in accessing it – or what is discussed here as 'improved experience'.

Netflix did not start from a deep library of owned IP and – since roughly 2014 – has tried to do something without precedent. Rather than seeing audiences outside the US as merely 'more scale', it has developed content in many different countries and built an exclusive segment of its library based on cross-distribution of that content rather than the one-way flow typical of the Hollywood export model. Of course a disproportionate amount of that content still comes from the US, but the percentage of content produced outside the country has tracked steadily with the increasing percentage of non-US subscribers in Netflix's overall subscriber base (see figure 2).[1] Netflix's current level of success is not simply because it is global; it is globally successful because of its strategy – which is the most

Figure 2 **Percentage of Netflix US subscribers and US commissions, 2015–2020**

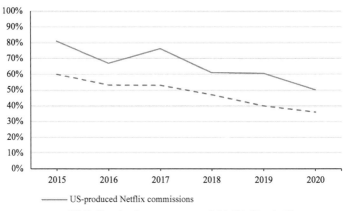

tailored among the global SVODs and addressed in detail in Part II. A multi-territory subscriber base exists for SVODs that can provide the right value proposition. But it is likely that the key to succeeding as a multi-territory service is to not imagine the globe as a monolithic market to which US conglomerates can push content that was developed for the strategic peculiarities of NBC's Monday-night schedule, a TNT original series, or even a movie likely to attract a large, heterogeneous audience to the cinema, as in the case of the owned-IP services. Companies that imagine multi-territory expansion is simply a matter of making the US library available outside the US may find recruiting and maintaining subscribers far more difficult than assumed.

Outside the US, potential subscribers may see more direct competition rather than complementarity among global services with predominantly US titles. Although Americans may be likely to subscribe to multiple

93

services, convincing people outside the US to pay for multiple 'US' SVODs is a tougher sell, and the scale needed to offset fading revenue from other distribution technologies for corporate extensions and to bankroll more commissioning requires subscribers outside the country. There is clearly a value proposition for one service – and, again, Apple and Amazon may coexist because they are more corporate complements than properly in the video business – but the competition among fairly substitutable services tightens quickly, especially considering the growing range of territory-specific SVODs and growing domestic on-demand options.

We've likely assumed too often that technology was the biggest impediment to multi-territory distribution and consequently believed that internet distribution 'creates' a global market simply because of its technological capabilities. Indeed, this is an important affordance, but it is far from the only factor in recruiting subscribers from various countries to a particular service. It is easy to assume that all that is needed to achieve scale and to leverage IP libraries is the technological ability to push content developed for the US or a loosely 'global' audience. Or to presume that content doesn't need to be branded by anything other than what company produced it. But these are dubious presumptions.

We can start with the obvious ways this is short-sighted: countries and the people in them have different compositions of tastes and sensibilities. Country to country, everything from internet accessibility to the existing state of video services varies considerably. Though it is true that companies such as Disney and Warner Bros. have earned billions over the years by selling the shows they've made to channels around the world, those shows were strategically selected by broadcasters familiar with the local market, and they were offered as part of a schedule built to attract a mass audience to sell to advertisers. Broadcasters with local expertise strategically selected and curated titles and used market expertise to schedule and promote them as well.

Netflix developed without its own library of owned content, so it doesn't have legacy IP created for another business or distribution model. It is still predominantly recognizable as a 'US' service, but it is significantly and intentionally more global in design than the other multi-territory SVODs. As discussed in chapter 8, the majority of titles in national Netflix libraries are produced outside the US – including in the US library. In terms of commissioning, as of December 2020, US commissions accounted for 61 per cent of its total commissions and, as figure 2 shows, is in decline.[2] But nearly all those commissions were created with the particular business of being a global SVOD in mind, and what it does license is strategically selected and curated for such a service. It may have started with pretty general licensing deals for packages of old titles, but over the last decade Netflix has deliberately refined what it buys to have an intentionally selected collection of titles related to its deep intelligence about taste clusters and their scale.

The key point here is to appreciate that geographic scale is an important governor on programme strategy. The more specialized the content offered by a service, the more geographic scale it needs, unless the 'specialization' derives from national specificity, as in the case of the single-territory service. Services without geographic scale require content distinct from what is otherwise available and need to be able to tap strong passion for content.

Services with specific libraries

Whether charting similarities among SVODs or Netflix's difference, this book barely attends to the situation of SVODs offering a specific form of content or single-territory service. Although characteristics from different 'reels', these attributes have a similar effect of limiting audience scale, which make these SVODs very different from the ones discussed thus far. The core components of subscriber funding and non-linear delivery remain the same, but such services attempt to trade the advantages that come from scale for passion. They can succeed only by offering something highly valued and otherwise un- or under-available.

Specific SVODs are complements to both linear services and global/general SVODs in the marketplace. Companies with owned IP tend not to offer specific SVODs because their IP was developed for the mass market prioritized by pre-digital distribution technologies. Specific SVODs also tend not to be corporate complements because an effective corporate complement provides value to the many rather than the few.

The sustainability equation for an SVOD requires balancing the scale of subscribers and their payment level with a content budget that will maintain that scale. Part of the reason Netflix must spend so much on content is because it competes within two large-scale markets – it competes as both a global service and a general service. It needs a library of a certain breadth and depth to allow it to take advantage of its scale. Thus, it may spend billions yearly, but it spends those billions on content from multiple countries and in several genres. In exploring the dynamic of geographic scale, Lobato and I (2021) considered Netflix's 2019 budget of US$15 billion at a per-subscriber level – Netflix's spending amounted to $100.80 per subscriber. In contrast, if a single-territory service such as the Australian service Stan spent at the same rate for its 2.2 million subscribers, it would amount to a total content budget of US$221.7 million (Stan's full reported expenses for 2020 were $156.9 million with revenues of $192.5 million).[3] It is a high level, but not wildly unattainable. Moreover, the key for single-territory and specific services isn't matching Netflix's budget, merely offering a library of content that maintains subscribers for less than the net revenue from those subscribers.

Crunchyroll is probably the most successful global, specific SVOD to date. The service offers anime to subscribers in many countries and is a perfect illustration of a content type largely absent from linear ad-supported video (at least outside Asia) for which strong, though not mass, interest exists. The SVOD part of the service surpassed 4 million subscribers in January 2021, soon after it was acquired by Sony for US$1.2 billion.[4] How can a service with only 4 million subscribers succeed or compel such an acquisition? In the same way both Hollywood blockbusters and low-budget films can succeed; specific SVODs don't need to match the revenue of global/general services, they just need to cover their costs.

The cost of content and the amount subscribers will pay for content are not fixed – different types of content have different costs and subscribers have different price points depending on how passionate they are about the content. The key levers here are the content budget – licensing anime and even commissioning is generally cheaper than live-action drama. Crunchyroll also has a smaller library – less than a fifth of the number of titles as Netflix in January 2021 – but speciality services can provide much more value to subscribers with far fewer titles. Consider arthouse film service Mubi, which offers only thirty films at a time but adds and drops a film daily. This strategy limits the library costs by directing its subscribers to a narrower but constantly evolving library. The rotation of the library compels viewers towards particular titles while reducing library cost. This strategy can work because of the specificity of the offering – those who subscribe to Mubi seek arthouse and classic film and are committed to the narrow range and curated experience it offers. Mubi's subscribers in their entirety are arguably comparable to a single Netflix taste cluster, though Mubi's library offers greater depth than would be found in a general service and arthouse isn't a taste cluster Netflix prioritizes. Mubi subscribers also don't expect it to provide something to watch with 'the family' or the latest blockbuster release. By tuning its offering with such specificity, it can balance costs and revenue. Such services can also use different licensing practices, such as a lower licence fee and paying per view. Often these services offer titles neither strongly in demand nor owned by major entertainment conglomerates, so licence holders may be more willing to collaborate and identify symbiosis than in the case of blockbuster titles, which need to recoup millions in costs.

The other lever is the cost of the service. A library that offers highly valued content can demand a higher fee relative to the number of titles if that content is particularly valued and subscribers have a sense of being able to find something to watch whenever they want – which might not be daily, or even weekly. The specialty services discussed here are priced comparably: Crunchyroll costs 1 dollar less (AU$10) than a standard Netflix subscription (monthly, in Australia) and Mubi 1 dollar more. But that needn't be the case. Perhaps the easiest place to see the dynamic of how passion will support significant subscriber fees is within sport. Fans of boxing have paid ample sums to watch single matches, while, in other cases, sports leagues or teams have been able to compel high payment for access to particular matches or events through special satellite channel packages.

Sport is a rapidly developing sector of SVOD and a complicated one. In the case of major sports within a country, linear ad-supported services are still willing to pay leagues significant licensing fees for exclusive access. These events generate sizable audiences and encourage live viewing, characteristics well suited to the features of linear delivery and ad-funding typical of these video providers. With a few experiments and exceptions, SVOD is not (yet) a more lucrative alternative for the conditions of major sports in their home country. However, SVOD can offer opportunity for smaller sports that are unlikely to win licensing deals or for sports outside their primary national market. For example, the National Football League dominates US sport viewing but isn't popular enough outside America to warrant linear licensing in most countries. However, the NFL offers the NFL Game Pass SVOD service for fans in many countries outside the US that extend access to its games, NFL Network, NFL RedZone, and other content. This service is not available in the US because linear ad-funded channels or domestic SVODs have secured exclusive rights. Before internet distribution, there was no way to service or monetize the limited interest that existed for minor sport or sport outside regions where it could earn linear licensing deals. SVODs thus might be a feasible tool to serve such audiences.

Contrast this with the scenario of a sport with multinational popularity such as what the rest of the world calls football. Multiple leagues draw multinational attention which makes linear rights valuable across national markets. Yet there remain countries in which linear licensing is difficult because of time zones or fewer fans (for example, European football matches generally air between 10 pm and 6 am in Australia). In these countries, an SVOD option presents a way to monetize the sport in a place where no linear rights revenue may have been generated. Moreover, a sports fan (or fan of any kind of content) is often willing to pay at higher levels than they would to support general content. This is the satisfaction coefficient, described in chapters 3, 8 and 9, that recognizes how quantity of content is not the only measure of an SVOD's value to a subscriber evaluating the worth of a subscription.

Having the technological capability to make minor sports available by SVOD isn't enough to make these ventures sustainable. There has to be enough interest to warrant the infrastructure costs. Few single sport SVODs have emerged, largely because the fixed costs of the enterprise aren't easily monetized. Rather, sport with fanbases too small for linear ad-supported licensing have been aggregated by sports SVODs such as Fubo (US), DaZN (multi), and Kayo (AU). Such services attempt to aggregate enough subscribers through a multiplicity of niche offerings to support their enterprise. Unlike most non-sports SVODs, they offer considerable linear content (a more complicated and costly infrastructure) and are funded through a blend of subscriber fees and advertising. To some extent, World Wrestling Entertainment illustrated the possibility of the exclusive single sport SVOD with its WWE Network that was the global source of content for fans (WWE Network became a purely non-US service in 2021, when rights to its content in the US were acquired by Peacock). The characteristics of wrestling entertainment – able to attract sizable audiences drawn from a passionate fanbase but with content that often made advertisers uneasy – was well suited to SVOD experiment. It was also privately held and didn't have a structure of multiple owners of distinct teams as in many sports. The service peaked at just 1.8 million subscribers, likely illustrating the challenge of maintaining enough content to provide a value proposition that satisfied subscribers.[5]

Single-territory SVODs

Another category of specific SVOD is the single-territory SVOD. This sector is difficult to theorize generally because such services tend to respond to specific national dynamics. For example, Hulu is one of the most significant single-territory services; however, it is most uncommon in its origins as a pooled effort of three major content conglomerates and largely just reproduces what would be catch-up services in most other countries.[6] Many single-territory SVODs are derived from and interconnected with existing linear companies in a way that makes them difficult to evaluate as a distinctive service without detailed market expertise (e.g. Blim [Mexico]). The Australian service Stan is useful for exploring many features that may suggest a prototype of single-territory SVODs and the challenges they face.

Stan offers a mix of scripted fiction series and movies with some documentary and a few reality/factual titles – 2,770 titles as of January 2021, roughly half the number of titles in the Netflix Australia library. It was launched by Nine Entertainment, the owner of the dominant commercial broadcast channel, but the company clearly distinguished Stan from the outset – at no point has it seemed tied to Nine or its IP in the manner of the US-based owned-IP services. This is likely the result of Nine producing few of its series internally and lacking IP rights. The titles Stan licenses from the US are probably not as targeted to taste clusters as Netflix's, but its strategy appears to focus on acquiring edgy titles distinct from those likely to air on Australian linear services – or, obviously, Netflix. In 2021, Stan's US-licensed titles accounted for 62 per cent of its library – many emblazoned with the promotional branding of 'Stan Exclusive' – and offered a mix of titles commissioned primarily by US cable channels or SVODs, noted in Nine's 2020 Annual Report as coming from sixteen different studios and distributors. Titles commissioned by Showtime and Hulu were strongly promoted by the service.

Although Stan has done well in Australia, ranking as the second most-subscribed SVOD, with 2.2 million subscribers in 2020 (behind Netflix at an estimated 6 million), the long-term viability of such a service is unclear, at least in its current form. Much like the reality once facing Netflix, access to the US IP Stan features has begun to shrink as American content conglomerates launch global SVODs. Stan offers primarily US content another route into Australia and was the home of Disney content before the launch of Disney+. Like the competing domestic service Binge, which is owned by Australia's monopoly cable provider Foxtel and has an output deal with HBO/Warner Bros., Stan has had a deal with CBS since 2014. That arrangement has been under pressure since CBS launched its 10 All Access SVOD (similar to CBS All Access) in Australia in 2019, but more so as CBS becomes more aggressive in its global offering and rebrands 10 All Access as Paramount+ (notably, CBS owns Australia's linear broadcast channel Ten). Stan has commissioned content since its launch, though totalled only twenty commissions in its library after six years. It announced an aggressive plan to commission thirty titles a year for five years beginning in 2021.[7]

Perhaps in parallel to Netflix's phased development, we may be experiencing Stan 1.0, in which it gains a firm foot in the marketplace by offering US titles not available from widely subscribed Netflix, only to pivot soon if US content becomes unavailable. Stan 2.0 might then rely more on commissioned Australian content bespoke to the service, productions of other single-territory SVODs and other foreign content, and licensed Australian content. The number of Australian-created titles in the Stan library nearly doubled between March 2019 and January 2021 (notably, the service's library size grew by 30 per cent in the same period), although Australian titles still account for only 7.4 per cent. Stan offers the most home-grown content of any

Australian service, but the leading national SVODs in other countries feature much higher percentages of domestic content.[8]

Single-territory SVODs face many challenges. There is considerable ability to differentiate from the general global services and exist as a complement, but the single-territory scale limits subscribers, and thus revenue. The extent to which these services can afford to create new domestic content is unclear and significantly dependent on adoption and country scale. It is also unclear how extensive demand for access to older domestic titles may be. The extent to which US companies conglomerated in the 1990s set them up well for the new competitive dynamics. Few countries allowed such concentration among channels and production companies, which means access to a substantive library of owned IP is rarely as accessible elsewhere. Here we see that analogue-era norms and policy that prioritized decentralized production sectors have unanticipated consequences. For example, in the UK, policy changes in 2003 required broadcasters to source a percentage of commissions from 'independent' producers.[9] As a result, many channels don't have the extent of self-owned IP that has enabled the US owned-IP extensions to come quickly to market. Owned IP allows services a preliminary value proposition that is low cost to the service but useful to establish a subscriber base and revenue in order to build a more bespoke offering. In many other places, libraries just aren't nearly so deep as those held by US conglomerates. Smaller countries have not been able to commission the same level of drama as those able to export and earn revenues supporting new production for large populations. Such nuanced analysis reveals the contextual differences that affect how and why single-territory SVODs develop in some places but not others.

Even though success does not require the scale of a general service or multi-territory or global reach, the cases of specific SVODs that seem solid and sustainable are not easy to emulate. It is their difference, their distinction, that makes them viable. The field is highly dynamic; what was different in 2018 isn't necessarily different in 2022, and who can guess where the market might be in 2025 and beyond. Specific SVODs clearly must offer content that some audiences embrace with considerable passion – as with a lot of sport and speciality genres. Or a distinct value proposition, such as territory-specific content, may be adequate. The viability of these services depends on the scale they can amass. Specific SVODs may find needed scale across national borders, while small and mid-sized countries might provide enough scale for a single-territory service aimed at national cultural specificity. The key is appreciating that necessary scale varies dependent on the service, and there is no need for all services to tread the same path.

6

The Discrepant Field of Global Services[1]

The state of 'competition' among SVODs depends a lot on where you are. It is impossible to catalogue the range of single-territory SVODs that are often critical to the viewers that access them. To keep this discussion widely accessible, it focuses on SVODs with global or multi-territory scale. With its long-in-market global reach of 240 million subscribers (January 2021), general library specificity, strategically licensed or bespoke IP, and pure play corporate position, Netflix dominates the category. Its global dominance may wane in time, but, for those seeking to understand the changing landscape of video ecosystems, Netflix offers many insights that are fascinating, though not clearly more widely applicable.

Just as there has been a tendency to conflate SVODs and linear ad-funded channels as a singular video market, there has been an inclination to assume all SVODs are engaged in a single competition. This is widely signalled in the press in the discourse of 'streaming wars'. I'm not suggesting there is *no* competition among these

106

services in identifying how they are differentiated by the different blends of the four structuring characteristics, rather, that the field is far more complicated than this paradigm assumes. We lose a lot of crucial nuance with simple frames of the market that lead to muddy understandings made worse by our unconscious adoption of the hegemonies of linear norms and demographic thinking. Instead of assuming all video distribution businesses are locked in a common battle in which one's success requires another's failure, let's think about another complicated competitive field in which variation is well understood and appreciated.

Cars come in many different shapes, sizes, categories, and price points. There are sedans, SUVs, and sports cars. Different cars are good at different things. If you haul a lot of goods, you'll want a light truck. A family of five has different needs from a young single person. No one would seriously suggest that Tesla will 'kill' Honda in the way the relation between Netflix and Disney+ has been discussed, or that separate markets for SUVs can't coexist with sports cars rather than one destroying the demand for the other.

But that's not all. In the same way that the desire for video news and entertainment is a broad enterprise, consider the broader market of transportation. Many needs might be handled by owning a car, others by public transit, walking, biking, electric scooter rental, or taxis and Ubers. These options aren't precise substitutes. Rather, they offer significant complementarity that meets the diverse needs of people to get around and their varying ability to pay to do so.

The ecosystem of video entertainment is similar. For some people, traditional linear television remains adequate, while others rely fully on internet-distributed services. Many cobble together a broad array of video services based on their different needs and ability to pay for them in money and time. Some services offer many titles and different types of content; others address very particular tastes. Some require viewers to pay a direct fee; others are advertiser supported; others still are supported with public funding.

Just as the emergence of electric scooters doesn't threaten to bring down the need for public transit, when assessing the twenty-first-century video distribution landscape, we need to account for the subtle differentiation of video services by revenue model, distribution technology, nature of content, intellectual property library, and primary aim of the service. The fact that Apple and Netflix both distribute video using the internet does not make them comparable or necessarily competitors. And the development of these companies that reproduce only a small portion of the kind of video we've called television is difficult to view as direct competition to multifaceted linear services that mostly measure success through a different metric. The purpose of an SVOD and that of a broadcaster is very different, just as the purpose of those broadcast channels was quite different from the video rental store.

Global SVODs are a complement to, not a replacement for, national broadcast television services. They provide an affordable, convenient way to view but do not – and never will – produce the array of programming people expect and desire. Moreover, they will never be able to afford the depth of production across countries that would be needed to *replace* national services. Their on-demand accessibility and subscriber funding allow them to offer a superior experience to linear video service, but they require payment. They may not be able to offer a depth of national content for many of the countries in which they operate, but they have provided an alternative source and superior experience, at least for the type of US-produced content that was already a significant part of channel schedules in many countries.

Netflix, in particular, also offers far more cross-nation content flow and discoverability than other distribution technologies or SVOD services, an attribute unusual among those commonly framed as competing services. It is also complementary in offering a lot of content distinctive from typical US fare. I wouldn't argue that Netflix commissions are 'better' than series commissioned by US channels, but they are notably different – as the chapters in Part II explore. Netflix's value proposition derives from offering convenient access to distinctive US content and providing a compelling array of multi-territory drama production – much of which services tastes and sensibilities that are infeasible for national channels to service affordably.

Understanding SVODs as a complement also suits the difference in revenue model and related metrics of success. Just as an expansion of a public transit system may lead many daily drivers to reassess their transportation needs, the option of Netflix and other SVODs pulls attention away from ad-funded services. But they do not directly affect the ad-funded market. Economically, ad-supported and subscriber-funded video are in distinct markets. Netflix and other SVODs don't threaten to take ad spending away from ad-supported broadcasters. They decrease the available supply of attention but, paradoxically, by reducing the attention available to advertisers, they make the remaining attention more valuable – decreased supply leads to higher pricing – so long as advertisers' demand holds constant.[2] (In many cases, demand has not held constant because advertisers have new options from search and social media.)

SVODs are changing video ecosystems, but zero-sum frames of 'wars' miss the complementarity. Most linear services will need to adjust strategies to persist. The number of channels may contract; they might not be as profitable; they may not have the cultural power that was once the case. But they also may innovate to play new and unexpected roles.

Netflix and other SVODs do bring new choices to viewers long dissatisfied by the value proposition of cable and satellite services that were driven by the same economic dynamics as linear ad-supported broadcasting and not motivated to innovate or service viewers in other ways. Still, it is difficult to say they 'compete' directly in the manner commonly implied. Perhaps it is more akin to the way ride-sharing poses an alternative to buying a second car in a family. It isn't exactly the same but might be a 'good enough' option for some. SVODs' complementary status is facilitated by the fact that nearly all linear service is ad-funded and thus paid for with viewers' time and hidden in the monetary economy.

Thinking in terms of complements rather than competition makes it easier to comprehend the complexity of video ecosystems that are likely to be multifaceted for a long time to come. Moreover, just as scooters and cars aren't subject to the same rules, even though both are forms of transportation, different types of video services warrant different policy approaches and considerations.

This transportation metaphor inspires a different frame of thinking and illustrates how Netflix, AppleTV+, and Amazon Prime Video might all 'win' the 'streaming war' because they are actually running different races

– or, to extend the metaphor properly, fighting different wars. The differentiation among the global, general library services means that Netflix's success as a pure play service leaves plenty of opportunity for other SVODs, especially given that others have different primary goals. A service such as AppleTV+ succeeds if Apple finds that it adds value to device buyers. Apple doesn't really care if you watch its shows; it wants you to buy its technology. The content production and distribution businesses return pennies of profit in comparison with the dollars of Apple device sales. Apple isn't trying to take over entertainment; it is securing a distinction from other technology manufacturers and diversifying its revenue.

The case is similar with Amazon. The core revenue there is the much broader retail business. Prime Video is offered as a value add-on with Prime membership because the latter boosts retail revenue and Amazon's retail share, which also helps drive its advertising business (the money that goods sellers spend to be prioritized in Amazon search and display). In countries without much of a retail service, Prime Video establishes a brand and relationship with little cost to the company in places where that retail service might someday expand. It's the first wave of colonization. Amazon Prime Video's commissioning is primarily in countries with a strong Amazon retail operation, and the size of its libraries varies substantially more by country than that of other services. Because the underlying reason for the existence of Netflix and Amazon Prime Video – the very reason they offer video – differs, so too do many of their aims and measures of success.

Disney+ is more difficult to situate. It is far more similar to Netflix than the others, but there are significant differences. Disney+ offers the company a way to monetize an existing library of intellectual property. It is not yet strategically developing a distinctive content experience through its SVOD service – although the Disney, Marvel, and Star Wars brands are well established. The bigger differences derive from the extent to which Disney is far more than just a video service. There is great synergy among its theme park, merchandise, and content, and the SVOD service only strengthens this as a point of connection with consumers. But it is also the case that, as a result, the core aims and priorities of Disney+ will differ from those of Netflix. And notably, even in cases in which these services may be running the same race, they are not clearly substitutable. To go back to the transportation metaphor, adding Disney+ may be like buying a bike when you already have a car (Netflix).

To some degree, many of the corporate complements (Disney+, Paramount+, Peacock) 'compete' not only with each other and Netflix but also with the other ways their parent companies earn money within the international market. They struggle to assess whether revenues from the streaming services will compensate for contracting licensing fees earned from individual national distributors (channels) as that business changes. And it isn't clear that all of the competitors in the US streaming war have sights on markets outside the US. One of the riskiest bits of Disney+'s gamble is that its multi-territory launch required it to end other licensing deals around the globe that delivered reliable revenue. In contrast, HBO expanded deals with several 'home of HBO' distributors in 2019 that allow HBO Max to take a more blended approach (at least through 2025) – launching HBO Max in some places but maintaining licensing deals in others. For example, Australian company Foxtel acquired the rights for the content on HBO Max and folded the HBO content into its domestic SVOD Binge. HBO Max is not available in Australia, the UK, Germany, or Italy, though it is in many other parts of the world. In another case, Peacock's foreign prospects are also unclear as its go-to-market strategy focused on ad sales that encourage a local market. Importantly, Peacock's corporate owner, Comcast, may be using the service in support of a different aim than video service alone. Comcast is competing for internet subscribers in the US: video is a battle strategy, but it is not the war. Comcast earns most of its money from delivering internet service in the US, which may be less glamorous than commissioning and distributing video, but it is much more lucrative and a business limited to the US (although Comcast also now owns satellite service Sky). Peacock may be more like Amazon Prime Video and Apple TV+, video services that exist as corporate complements in pursuit of a goal other than providing video to subscribers.

Other SVOD services may have the same underlying characteristics of on-demand access, subscriber funding, and the capacity for simultaneous multi-territory release, but no others have anything like Netflix's scale of multi-territory commissioning and licensing. Elsewhere, I've described Netflix as a zebra among horses.[3] A more expansive analysis of the internet-distributed video market might necessitate an array of animals from the genus equus to attend to the meaningful differences among services – i.e., YouTube is a donkey, Amazon Prime Video a mountain zebra, and so on – in order to properly conceptualize the similarity and yet considerable variety. Of course funding source is a key distinction; after that, multi-territory scale and whether the service owns a substantial library of intellectual property provide other key distinctions, as the slot machine in figure 1 and its various reels illustrate.

Painting all 'streamers' or SVOD services in a single category – as the 'streaming wars' frame common in the US does – also obscures the significant differences among the underlying licensing terms that differentiate services. Although my years of constant thinking on these matters allow me to dissect the marketplace with surgical precision, it is crucial to remember how these services started and gradually evolved, and delimit viewers' acculturation with this new ecosystem in ways very different than those seen with an industrial lens. The industrial features of those originally identified as 'catch-up services' were once quite different from SVODs.[4] General viewers can hardly be expected to understand the variation in underlying economics of an SVOD and a catch-up service. These services seem the same when national debates emerge about how to manage the video ecosystem. But, industrially, much of the content on a catch-up service is based on a linear commissioning window agreement that creates different economics and circumscribes the programme strategies they can adopt.

The general point here is to re-establish the assertion made in the introduction that 'provides video' is a poor market boundary, 'provides video by internet' lumps together services with quite different aims, and even the SVOD sector contains significant internal variation. The persistence of frames such as 'streaming wars' obscures the complementarity in offerings and the very complicated differentiation among business models that are the foundation of SVODs. Rather than the field of video competition commonly assumed, the multifaceted ecosystem requires more sophisticated sorting to appreciate the twenty-first-century video context.

In contrasting these services and their characteristics, Netflix stands apart because it is a pure play service endemic to internet distribution. It did not have a legacy content business in the way characteristic of most others able to launch on a global scale. As a pure play service, Netflix focuses on one thing – providing video to subscribers. Although its strategy is not the only way to design an SVOD, its single purpose ensures that its actions are based on a goal of compelling viewers to subscribe to a video service.

The other crucial distinction is that Netflix lacked owned IP at the start. As of 2022, its national libraries blend licensed and bespoke content, and bespoke content now accounts for roughly a quarter of national libraries. Starting from zero owned IP and its absence from the business of producing content for other commissioners – as the case of corporate extensions – also differentiate Netflix from other global services. These features enable assessment of its content strategy without needing to factor how a desire to leverage content in other venues – such as cable channels or in theatrical release – might affect its content strategy.

Part I Conclusion

As these chapters illustrate, SVODs are different from linear ad-supported services, often in pretty profound ways. When I started writing about SVODs in 2015 (*Portals*, published 2017), I did advocate considering a service such as Netflix as internet-distributed 'television'. Understandings were significantly less nuanced at that time, and many different kinds of internet video services were commonly conflated. In those days, the pervasive belief was that anything distributed by 'the internet' was 'new media' and thus radically different from existing video industries. It was necessary then to explain how and why YouTube and Netflix are very different things, while now that seems apparent, even to general users.

At that time, most of Netflix's streaming library was composed of series commissioned for broadcast and cable television, many from long before internet-distributed video was even imagined. And it was mostly a US service. Consequently, Netflix seemed clearly to be offering 'television' and movies, not 'web series'[1] – a term some suggested. The assumption that video distributed using the internet was categorically different from video distributed using other technologies seemed wholly wrong to me. This framing obscured the profound similarities among video – regardless of distribution technology – and hid the great extent to which 'video' and the practices of its production remained constant – again, at that time.

But, since then, commissioned titles have grown in importance to Netflix's overall strategy, and the SVOD market and its use have expanded considerably. From the vantage point of the viewer, series commissions do have much in common with television; however, the chapters here illustrate how many aspects 'behind the scenes' make the motivations of SVODs very different. Claiming Netflix as television in 2016 was also an emotional response to the assumptions and claims of television's impending death that were pervasive earlier in this century, despite its being clear something the opposite of dying was happening. The old hegemonies were being challenged, and to many that looked like death. But I also saw industrial features coming into place that could finally allow US television to be something different from what it had been and was wary of allowing television to be replaced with a term so vacant of specific meaning as 'web series'.

I had reasons for once arguing Netflix – the pioneer SVOD – as internet-distributed television, but, if I could go back, I'd reframe *Portals* as about 'internet-distributed video' – especially in terms of commissioned titles. Although there is considerable formal similarity in the content commissioned by linear ad-supported channels and SVODs, the nature of this content, the strategic purpose of the content to different services, and the strategies by which they pursue that purpose are critically different.

Also, 'television' has always been far more than the scripted fiction series my research has focused on. Television is also morning talk shows, news, game shows, sports, and an assortment of light entertainment. SVODs offer a relatively small amount of the array of content we have known as television. As of 2022, mass-market SVODs really overlap only with scripted series and movies, although there are some attempting more specific offerings in sports, reality, and factual programming. Thinking of SVODs as television is poorly justified in terms not only of their economics and technology but also in relation to their programming.

SVODs have emerged as a largely superior video service for scripted fiction series and out-of-theatre movie distribution. Ironically, much of the programming general SVODs deliver quite successfully – drama, documentary, children's – was regarded as 'market failure' forms for the norms of linear ad-supported channels outside the countries that had the wealth and scale to support ample series production domestically. Yet because drama, children's television, and documentaries are regarded as highly culturally valuable, many channels struggle to produce them due to the costs relative to the revenue they produce in a linear ad-supported environment. Because we'd known only the conditions of linear television, many believed these *forms* were market failures, but it was just that they were poorly suited to *linear ad-supported delivery*. They are much better aligned with the strategies of a subscriber-funded service able to deliver content on demand and build scale among more specific taste clusters with multinational reach (or to non-commercial motives of public funding).

Part I Conclusion

In a world of only analogue technology, television industries – often with regulatory prodding and the support of nations – found a way to deliver these supposed market failure forms even though it was like forcing a square peg into a round hole. Rather than continuing that struggle and expecting the same of all services, industries, creators, and viewers are better served by allowing the services to differentiate types of content based on what their industrial features best suit them to deliver.

SVODs and linear ad-supported channels are not as comparable as has been widely presumed. The commonality of offering video is not enough to claim a shared competitive field, as indicated by the many facets discussed in the last chapter. But it is the case that SVODs, as well as other forms of digital distribution such as the additional broadcast channels made available by digital transmission and catch-up services, have also fundamentally altered the competitive dynamics of video service from the start of the century. The introduction of all these digital technologies has enabled innovation and has disrupted the ability of linear ad-supported channels to maintain previous practices. The relationship of the video ecosystem is too complex to frame everything as simple competition.

Part I of the book aimed to address the general dynamics of SVODs, even though this sector encompasses video services with considerable variety. There are key ways SVODs differ from the linear ad-supported norms that have largely governed thinking about in-home video viewing, and appreciating those distinctions is a crucial starting point for understanding the twenty-first-century video ecosystem.

PART II

Netflix is Not Like Other Subscriber-Funded Streaming Video Services

7

Netflix Content Concepts and Vocabulary

Part II focuses on Netflix, a very particular and peculiar SVOD, at least as of 2022. Given its early market status and phenomenal global take-up, Netflix is often perceived as representative or typical of the entire SVOD category, and this is simply not the case. The mixing of the four structuring characteristics (table 1) highlight Netflix's atypicality. In much reporting about SVODs, there is a tacit presumption that these services already are, or will become, consistent in strategy and aim. But the differences in their structuring characteristics suggest why we shouldn't expect that to be the case. As Part I indicates, there is a fair bit that can be said about SVODs and how they are distinct from linear ad-supported television or theatrical distribution, but the following chapters illustrate how Netflix's blend of characteristics leads it to be quite distinctive from other SVODs.

Netflix's industrial characteristics enable particular content strategies at the level both of the library and of the individual titles that compose that library. Those

who have done detailed reporting informed by interviews with those working at Netflix – particularly Josef
Adalian[1] and Brian Barrett[2] – have dropped hints of
the different concepts Netflix has employed to build its
libraries (the plural here because Netflix subscribers in
different countries access bespoke national libraries).
Rarely are these words defined in much detail; this
part of the book uses extensive reading of interviews
by Netflix executives, investor documents, and media
coverage to ground speculative understanding.

Verticals categorize types of content. Adalian explains
these as 'super-specific genres of film and television,
such as young-adult comedies, period romances, or
sci-fi adventures.' *Verticals are a general classification of
content.* Indeed, they are more specific than comedy or
drama – words that might be used to distinguish content
offered by linear services or for theatrical release – but
verticals are still pretty blunt categorizations and not far
removed from what services based on other distribution
technologies might use.

The *taste cluster* is a concept that appears in both
Barrett's and Adalian's articles and in a variety of
interviews with Netflix executives. *A taste cluster is
also a group of texts, but its boundaries are established
using analysis of viewing patterns rather than textual
traits* (although textual traits may explain the viewing
patterns). There is likely overlap between verticals
and taste clusters, but clusters are titles connected by
common viewership that can transcend the textual
features used in classifying titles by vertical. Taste
clusters cannot be derived from content features alone.
A single taste cluster may include shows in very different
verticals because they are often watched by the same
viewers. One of the most succinct explanations comes

from Barrett, who describes them as *groupings of titles based on what subscribers like*, noting, 'Netflix assigns each subscriber three to five of these clusters, weighted by the degree to which each matches their taste.' Taste clusters have not existed previously because there has not been a way to systematically track viewing behaviour across titles.

I imagine Netflix identifying my taste clusters by comparing everything I watch on the service in the context of the titles viewed by its other millions of viewers. Adalian's article includes an explanation from Olivia De Carlo, a director on Netflix's commissioned series launch team, who explains that it begins from identifying patterns, and showed Adalian a chart depicting how subscribers who liked *Black Mirror* were also fans of *Lost* and *Groundhog Day*. From Adalian:

'On the surface, if you thought about *Groundhog Day* with *Black Mirror*, you might not find an obvious similarity,' De Carlo tells the group. '*Lost* and *Black Mirror* is also a stretch. But when you look at these in aggregate, you can see this through-line of supernatural or extreme worlds, and somehow that clustering tends to make more sense.' She then points to another graphic detailing other shows and movies that 'have this dark-drama through-line,' and spells out what it means to the Netflix recommendation engine. 'If a member hasn't yet watched *Black Mirror* but they've watched *Shameless* and *Orphan Black* and *The OA*, we can be relatively confident in suggesting *Black Mirror* to them,' De Carlo says.

How do these taste clusters guide Netflix? These groupings offer hints of alternative schemes of title classification derived from viewership rather than story characteristics. This data helps Netflix recommend more precisely and can help inform decisions about what shows to develop or license based on those largely invisible intersections. For example, I suspect there is some link between my taste for cynical mom-coms (*Workin' Moms*; *Better Things*; *The Letdown*) and dark, complicated political drama (*Borgen*; *Occupied*), although such titles would be organized into very different verticals. I might have trouble recognizing a series that fits that intersection as something I'd like, but Netflix might be able to use the viewing patterns of millions of others to create those links and make the recommendation.

If taste clusters are intersections of titles, we can imagine *taste communities* as *aggregations of people around particular types of titles in those clusters*. Importantly, taste communities derive from what we watch; our behaviour sorts us into taste communities, which is somewhat the reverse of how programmers have used demographic features as indicative of people's likelihood to view – a behaviour. Ashley Rodriguez reported on a Netflix press release in 2016 announcing that the service had shifted to understanding these communities as '*global*'.[3] At that point Netflix discussed the existence of some 1,300 taste communities, including fans of a subset of anime titles or healthfood-conscious documentary viewers, and those communities weren't bound within national borders. The terminology of taste communities appears in Netflix coverage, but how they are derived and how they relate to taste clusters or verticals is not clear (both the examples from Rodriguez's article seem defined more by a sub-vertical than a taste cluster). A couple of key things to keep in mind in terms of how Netflix claims to use these concepts:

people belong to more than one taste community, and the reported number of them has ranged from 1,300 to 2,000 micro-clusters.

To be clear, taste clusters and taste communities are different again from the 'altgenres' Alex Madrigal reported in an early article focused on Netflix movie categorization.[4] That was certainly a starting point, but the classification system has evolved. Madrigal's project reverse-engineered Netflix recommendations circa 2014 and identified that the service had 76,897 unique ways to describe types of movies. The Netflix altgenres were built on a carefully trained team watching movies and tagging them with metadata about features such as 'sexually suggestive content, goriness, romance levels, and even narrative elements like plot conclusiveness'. Undoubtedly, some of these features have been flattened into the publicly facing category of 'tone'; Netflix includes two or three words describing tone in the library metadata provided for each commissioned title. Many of the others probably persist in the background in the recommendation algorithm.

Significantly, Netflix can use this kind of 'intelligence' in its content strategy only *because it knows what people actually watch*. It doesn't know what Amanda Lotz watches, or that she's a forty-something Australian immigrant who often watches with her tweenagers or as part of professional curiosity about Netflix's multinational commissions. But just knowing that a viewer based in Australia devoured *Workin' Moms* and also watched *Glee*, *Money Heist*, and *Sacred Games* in a single month is unprecedented and important data and just one of the millions of viewing profiles it can capture. The key learning of the system is that there is a connection between title A and title B, especially if that connection shows up repeatedly. Its data has advantages of both precision (derived from behaviour, not self-reported) and scale. In contrast, theatrical distribution or linear ad-supported channels have only the most rudimentary knowledge about who watches titles, and that knowledge is organized in blunt demographic categories. Such services have no ability to develop a picture of how different preferences might align into clusters or communities, and that's not part of the strategy.[5] Instead, a linear ad-supported service simply seeks programmes likely to attract the kind of viewers advertisers desire (typically young, educated, and wealthy).

Concepts such as taste clusters and taste communities are very different from the vocabulary terms typical of linear ad-supported strategy. Among such services, content is often described in terms similar to 'verticals'; programmes might be divided generally as comedy, drama, reality, and then with a bit more specificity, such as police drama or family comedy. Instead, SVODs can offer targeted recommendations through personalized interfaces that suggest titles based on people's past viewing. But, importantly, the logic behind the recommendation is not to amass an audience for a particular title but to satisfy individuals based on known patterns of viewing.

In addition to the terms vertical, taste cluster, and taste community that come from Netflix, I'd like to add the word *'sensibility'* to the vocabulary used to discuss programme strategy. Sensibility describes a particular subscriber's taste or preferences (I'm using sensibility instead of taste because taste comes with a lot of baggage in some uses). Basically, your *sensibility is what you like – it is what puts you in particular taste communities*. When Netflix imagines the audience for a possible licensed or commissioned title, it does so by envisioning the sensibility the title serves, and it can do this with much greater nuance than a preference for general content types such as police drama or family comedy.

Your sensibility may lead you to prefer some verticals over others, but even within a preferred vertical you are likely to connect only with certain titles due to a fit with preferred tone and other characteristics that define your sensibility. Your sensibility leads you to become articulated in particular taste communities based on the intersection of your sensibility with the titles Netflix offers.

Along with sensibility, *tone* is a concept worth both considering in more depth and exploring beyond Netflix's tone designations, such as heartfelt, gritty, or goofy, that can be found in the series descriptions within the interface – although even these alone are revealing. If verticals categorize titles by types of narrative – what the title is about – tone categorizes how stories are told. There is a big difference between a drama that can be described as endearing or heart-warming and those that are ominous or suspenseful. Tone is a feeling word. The key difference between a story about a family that is dark and suspenseful and one that is heart-warming and inspiring is how those shows will make you feel. In selecting content, Netflix isn't simply attending to different types of content but also ensuring that its subscribers can service a range of states of escape. Tone descriptors are more sophisticated tools for categorizing our sensibilities; they enable Netflix to identify far more variation among programmes and identify which sensibilities can be serviced more particularly than the descriptions in content features would allow. I imagine that my sensibilities are better characterized by tone than by vertical, and I wonder to what extent taste clusters are more strongly determined by tone than content as well.

Tone is not a widely considered concept in media studies. Nearly all categorization of programming is based on content, story, or genre classifications. This is not the place to develop an extensive argument as to why, but in the case of television it most certainly derives considerably from the goals of building a mass audience and seeking a tone unlikely to diminish the breadth of viewers. Tone has been unremarked upon because it was so reliably unobtrusive.

Preferred tone intersects with preferred content type as the basis of one's sensibility. I first recognized tone in my own viewing when I found *Workin' Moms*, a title created for the Canadian Broadcasting Corporation that was a more honest depiction of the challenges of working motherhood than I'd ever seen. I wasn't looking for a show about being a mom; in fact, I'd say I would have actively refused a title described, as Netflix does, as 'Four new working mothers and friends deal with the struggles and nuttiness of returning to work while trying to balance their family and love lives.' But my viewing history led to its recommendation, something about the cover imagery led me to push play (I did *not* read the programme description at the time), and I found a story and characters that resonated.

The Netflix recommendation engine suggested other titles such as the Australian co-commission *The Letdown*, which was topically and thematically similar. These titles joined other commissioned series of which I'd watched at least a few episodes – *Unbreakable Kimmy Schmidt*, *Grace and Frankie*, and *Russian Doll*, as well as the licensed series *The Good Place* – to locate me in a taste cluster (or so I'm guessing). It is a cluster based on my viewing; let's consider it the 'irreverent womanhood' cluster. The cluster crosses verticals (admittedly, I don't know how fine the vertical or altgenre-type categorizations Netflix uses are. *Workin' Moms* is classified only as 'TV Comedy' and 'Canadian TV Show' on the interface). Table 2 shows several series and movies comparing the tone descriptors Netflix lists and how I'd describe the vertical.

As I contemplated the commonality among these series, tone emerged as an important part of the categorization. These series tell different kinds of stories and are consistently about female characters in worlds in which the moral centre of the narrative deviates from what is typical in mainstream US linear ad-supported television. They may generally be 'comedies' but probably belong in a handful of different verticals. As I began to investigate the two tone words used to describe my favourite titles more systematically, it became clearer what was core to my sensibility and why I prefer comedies on Netflix (though not all Netflix comedies) to those I find on linear ad-supported channels. The tone words that appear along with my favourite comedies are quirky, witty, cynical, and raunchy. A lot of linear ad-supported comedy might be witty, but quirky pushes you to the edge of mass viability quickly, and cynical too is more likely a characteristic of a cable commission than what a US broadcaster might try (*Better Things* on FX illustrates the point). And cynical towards motherhood? Readers of a certain age will recall the condemnation laid on *Murphy Brown* (which actually wasn't cynical about motherhood, just about everything else) and *Roseanne* (the 1990s version). Sure, mothers in family comedies such as *Everyone Loves Raymond*, *Malcolm in the Middle*, and even

Netflix

Table 2 The 'irreverent womanhood' cluster

Title	Tone descriptors	Vertical
Commissioned/co-commissioned		
Workin' Moms	cynical; raunchy	working mom-com
Unbreakable Kimmy Schmidt	quirky; witty	single in the city comedy
Dead to Me	offbeat; witty	complicated female friends comedy
The Letdown	witty; intimate	working mom-com
Girl Boss	quirky; intimate single	woman comedy
Russian Doll	cynical; offbeat	comedy
Never Have I Ever	quirky; heartfelt	teen dramedy
Grace and Frankie	quirky; heartfelt	complicated female friends comedy
Gilmore Girls: A Year in the Life	witty; intimate	mother/daughter dramedy
Isn't It Romantic (M)	witty; irreverent	romantic comedy
Wine Country (M)	witty; irreverent	girls out comedy
Otherhood (M)	witty; feel-good	girls out comedy
Licensed		
The Good Place	quirky; witty	ensemble comedy
Great News	quirky; witty	single woman workplace comedy
Derry Girls	quirky; witty	teen girl friend comedy
Gilmore Girls	witty; intimate	mother/daughter dramedy
A Bad Mom's Christmas (M)	raunchy; irreverent	girls out comedy

This table captures an imagined taste cluster and dynamics of tone and vertical that delimit it.

Home Improvement were allowed to move beyond the idealized motherhood of previous decades. But raunchy or cynical mom-coms remain outside the content viable for constructing a mass audience.

Tone is a crucial distinction in comedy, but it also differentiates drama. Again, drawing on my own sensibility, dark and cerebral are tone words Netflix uses to describe two of my favourite commissioned dramas, as well as licensed titles such as *Breaking Bad*. In many ways, tone – again, how a story is told – is the unifying feature among a list of titles I like that are otherwise quite disparate. Notably, dark and cerebral are not words that characterize many US linear commissions, certainly not those of broadcast networks, and well explains my abiding fandom of the FX channel in the early 2000s.

These concepts of verticals, taste clusters, taste communities, and sensibilities provide the vocabulary necessary to discuss Netflix's content strategy. To be clear, the different industrial dynamics of SVODs – of creating libraries that bundle titles and selling access to the bundle for a flat fee – strongly differentiate them from linear ad-supported services. An SVOD such as Netflix has a holistic library strategy designed to optimize options for a range of sensibilities. It then services these sensibilities based on amassing a depth of content that provides value to a variety of taste clusters. Such strategies are well suited to helping SVODs offer content valued enough by viewers to compel their payment. And, because they are paying a flat fee, SVODs need not be driven to push viewers to the same titles in the manner of creating mass hits. The next two chapters explore Netflix's strategy first in how it aggregates programming into a library, and then the strategies that guide particular titles.

8
Netflix Library Strategies

Netflix's structuring SVOD characteristics enable its distinctive library strategy. The composition of its library has steadily changed over its fifteen years as a streaming service, so any effort to write about it merely captures a moment in time. Yet the current moment can be considered one of decent maturity. Netflix's start as a DVD-by-mail service based its origins in distributing licensed content, which is also how its streaming service began. Part of its strength as a DVD-by-mail service was the breadth of its library (enabled by US first-sale doctrine), and its general 'department store' approach can be placed in these roots. Netflix evolved from a service that aspired to offer every movie available on DVD and the type of television that was found in 'box sets'. Its contemporary focus on scripted series, movies, documentaries, and children's programming clearly ties to these roots rather than to an effort to reproduce 'television norms'. Although the Netflix library heavily emphasizes scripted fiction entertainment for adults, it offers many different types of entertainment, unlike a 'speciality' SVOD that would probably offer only one of these content types. In January 2021, children's and family programmes accounted for 14 per cent of the library, documentary for 7 per cent, and reality for 1 per cent. The remaining 78 per cent included scripted crime thrillers, comedies, romance, sci-fi, action, and horror titles.[1]

Elsewhere, I've periodized Netflix into three phases: Netflix 1.0 includes the DVD-by-mail enterprise; Netflix 2.0 marks the expansion into streaming, in which it offered an additional window for content and was bound to the US market; and Netflix 3.0 encompasses the nearly coterminous shift towards significant commissioning of titles and expanding to be a global service.[2] Netflix began commissioning series in 2011 and soon adopted a norm of acquiring long-term rights that create significant library stability among its commissioned titles. It transitioned from being a US service to a global one just a few years after this, so it is difficult to discern a clear strategy in its first years of commissioning beyond a notable and rarely discussed emphasis on children's and family titles (see table 3).[3] But, by 2021, both its commissioning and multinational practices had developed to offer some coherence.

As it launched libraries in other countries, Netflix devised a library composition formula that appears fairly consistent across major markets, although, as of 2021, the titles among the libraries were only roughly 60 per cent the same, at least across the libraries of seventeen of the countries with the most subscribers.[4] Comparing the ratio of commissioned to licensed titles and of foreign and domestic content, and also assessing the source of foreign content in national libraries, provides

Netflix

Table 3 Netflix's first commissions

Title	Release	Genre	Primary Production Country
House of Cards (US)	Feb-13	Drama	USA
Hemlock Grove	Apr-13	Crime & Thriller	USA
Arrested Development	May-13	Comedy	USA
Orange Is the New Black	Jul-13	Crime & Thriller	USA
Turbo Fast	Dec-13	Children & Family	USA
BoJack Horseman	Aug-14	Comedy	USA
Trailer Park Boys	Sep-14	Comedy	Canada
VeggieTales in the House	Nov-14	Children & Family	USA
Marco Polo	Dec-14	Action & Adventure	USA
All Hail King Julien	Dec-14	Children & Family	USA
The Adventures of Puss in Boots	Jan-15	Children & Family	USA
Ever After High	Feb-15	Children & Family	Canada
Richie Rich	Feb-15	Children & Family	USA
Unbreakable Kimmy Schmidt	Mar-15	Comedy	USA
Bloodline	Mar-15	Crime & Thriller	USA
Marvel's Daredevil	Apr-15	Action & Adventure	USA
H2O: Mermaid Adventures	May-15	Children & Family	France
Grace and Frankie	May-15	Comedy	USA
Sense8	Jun-15	Sci-Fi & Fantasy	USA
Wet Hot American Summer: First Day of Camp	Jul-15	Comedy	USA
Club De Cuervos	Aug-15	Comedy	Mexico
Project Mc²	Aug-15	Children & Family	USA
Dinotrux	Aug-15	Children & Family	USA
Narcos	Aug-15	Crime & Thriller	USA
Popples	Oct-15	Children & Family	USA
The Mr. Peabody and Sherman Show	Oct-15	Children & Family	USA
Care Bears and Cousins	Nov-15	Children & Family	USA
Master of None	Nov-15	Comedy	USA
W/ Bob & David	Nov-15	Comedy	USA
Marvel's Jessica Jones	Nov-15	Action & Adventure	USA

This table captures the first thirty Netflix commissions, many developed before the Netflix 3.0 pivot towards multinational reach and extensive commissioning.

a basic but useful way to appreciate the similarity and differences within the library strategy/strategies of the service. Netflix libraries are quite consistent in the ratio of commissioned to licensed titles, the ratio of domestic to foreign titles (though more variation here), and the ratio of movie to series titles.[5] As of 2021, the ratio of licensed titles to commissions was roughly 70:30 across the service, a consistency arising from fairly uniform library size across countries and because its commissions are available in nearly all libraries.[6] The ratio of foreign to domestic content varies; for most countries, less than 1 per cent of content is domestic. For the seventeen countries with high subscriber counts which we analysed, countries that collectively account for 80 per cent of subscribers, domestic content accounts for an average of 8 per cent. A few countries have much higher levels (US: 39 per cent; Japan: 24.1 per cent; South Korea: 13.8 per cent; India: 12.5 per cent), although US and Indian content account for the most titles in nearly all libraries. Across the libraries, series compose 32 to 39 per cent, while movies make up 61 to 68 per cent. The balance between series and movies is narrower for Netflix commissions, with series accounting for 52 to 54 per cent of libraries and movies 46 to 48 per cent.

A clear difference between Netflix's library strategy and that of other global SVODs is the extent to which its titles are from many countries. Where US productions compose 92 per cent of the Disney+ and AppleTV+ libraries and 50 per cent of Amazon Prime Video, US titles do not compose the majority in any Netflix library – including in the US.[7] Averaged across the seventeen countries in the analysis I undertook in collaboration with Eklund and Soroka, the US accounted for 41 per cent of the libraries, India 8.5 per cent, Japan 6 per cent, the UK 5.3 per cent, South Korea 4.8 per cent, and France 3.4 per cent.[8] As many as seventy-nine different countries appear as the origin of titles, but the ten largest contributors (the above, plus Spain, Canada, China, and Egypt) account for 79 per cent of library titles. In sum, Netflix titles are sourced from a greater diversity of places than is the case with other global SVODs, but the sources remain concentrated among a few countries. Nevertheless, Netflix offers a greater diversity of content sources than is typical of linear channels.

These ratios suggest two of the key differences of Netflix's library strategy relative to that of many other global SVODs: the extent to which it offers non-US content (roughly 60 per cent of libraries) and the extent to which it has commissioned titles specifically for its service. Netflix's sourcing of libraries from multiple countries is discussed in depth in chapter 10. The role of commissioning is consequently the focus here.

Over the last decade, Netflix placed a greater emphasis on commissions for reasons related to competitive dynamics and strategy. The initial reliance on licensed content was related to establishing an SVOD service – which was once very different from the established market of video services and regarded sceptically by the rest of the industry as well as consumers. It needed to build subscribers and revenue before endeavouring to commission content, which is very expensive and, historically, very risky. The familiarity of licensed titles was crucial when the service launched and SVODs were foreign to viewers. A library based on licensed titles also allowed Netflix to appear more as friend than a threat to those with which it would eventually compete. Steadily increasing commissions has been a strategic shift that enabled Netflix to craft its own identity/ identities and to prepare for a time when the companies from which it bought content, such as Disney, launched their own services. The scale at which Netflix commissions content is a key distinguishing characteristic at this point. Providing value to subscribers with commissioned titles prevented it from overreliance on content owners that might demand licensing fees that would challenge its business model.

Commissions are important because they allow Netflix to more precisely develop content with the characteristics strategically valuable to its service – to make sure there is enough in the library for the different sensibilities and taste clusters that subscribe. Exclusivity is another feature that makes commissioned titles particularly valuable to Netflix – or any SVOD. Being the only place to access a title – at least the only SVOD source – can be quite valuable to a service even in the case of licensed titles, and some titles might organically align with perceived library needs. Commissioning is also crucial for a service to enact the specific title level strategies discussed in the next chapter. SVODs that can only afford to license are limited to what others have produced based on other particular industry logics and strategies.[9]

To date, few SVODs have commissioned much content, and in many cases that content is in comparatively affordable genres such as stand-up comedy. Although hundreds of SVODs exist, according to the forty-eight major markets measured by Ampere Analysis at the time of our research, only twenty-six have commissioned scripted fiction content specifically for an SVOD service, and Netflix far exceeds its peers in 2022 (see figure 3).[10] As of this writing, Netflix has 1520

Netflix

Figure 3 Hours of commissions among a sample of SVODs

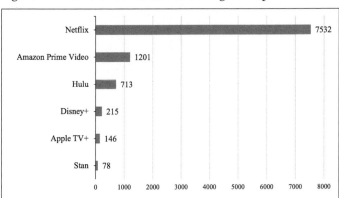

Netflix 7532
Amazon Prime Video 1201
Hulu 713
Disney+ 215
Apple TV+ 146
Stan 78

■ Hours of commissions

This figure indicates the substantial difference in the number of hours Netflix has commissioned for its service in comparison with other well-known SVODs. Based on 2021 Ampere Analysis data; apart from Stan, titles available in US library.

commissioned titles that account for roughly a third of what the service offers. Compare this with the commissions of other global SVODs indicated in table 1 (p. 10), although Netflix has been commissioning for an SVOD for a decade longer than nearly all these other services.

This language of commissions and licensed titles does not map perfectly across series and movies. Series reliably fall in these categories because they are not made without a commissioner; however, some of the movies Netflix acquires are exclusive to the service but are not 'commissioned' because they are independently financed or because a studio decides to skip a theatrical window. Such movies, for example *The Cloverfield Paradox* or *Tallulah*, were completed before Netflix acquired them, but Netflix acquired exclusive global

140

streaming rights. These movies are somewhat comparable to co-commissions in that they often appear to viewers as commissions because they were never otherwise available, and Netflix promotes them as 'originals'. Netflix acquires completed movies because it finds strong fit with a content strategy or broader purpose (attracting awards and buzz), but these titles are different since Netflix is unable to offer creative input. (The fact that a movie may appear for a limited time in theatres is nothing to make a big deal about. It is common with these acquisitions – especially outside the US – and can happen in the US simply to satisfy requirements for Oscar consideration. It does not suggest Netflix has an out-of-home strategy.)

The composition of Netflix's libraries has steadily changed over time from the service's origin of nearly all licensed US titles and will likely continue to do so. Linear services typically license programmes for a limited period because they are trying to drive viewership at specific times and regularly need new programmes to do so. In contrast, Netflix and other SVODs seek much longer availability of commissions as part of the distinction of 'building a library' rather than a schedule. New Netflix commissions aren't replacing old ones; rather, both new and old continue to exist in the library – at least for now. As Netflix produces more series, the ratio of its bespoke to licensed content will likely increase. Its aim of profitability encourages it to amortize commissioned titles as long as possible and to limit the cost of licensing titles to those offering clear and direct benefit to subscriber levels. It is less clear how significantly the ratio of US-produced licensed content will evolve. That probably depends on the success of the SVODs developed by major IP holders such as Disney,

WarnerMedia, Viacom, and Comcast and the extent to which they scale their services into the international market.

Looking past the Top 10

As it is skilled at doing, Netflix captured a flurry of unpaid publicity in early 2020 when it incorporated data about the daily Top 10 shows by country in users' recommendation screen. Since it is legendary for the lack of data it makes available, this seemed a wild change of course, and, within weeks, services such as FlixPatrol developed to aggregate the cross-national data and attempted to build something approximating a cumulative audience count. But what does knowing the ten most viewed titles in a country each day really tell us? The short answer: nothing.

The only consistent audience data Netflix has shared publicly is a daily list of the ten most watched shows by country, or, more precisely, the ten shows of which most people watched the first two minutes. These lists offer only ordinal indications and simply arrange the series with no sense of the intervals among the rankings or way of discerning whether the most viewed show on a Tuesday was seen by fewer than the lowest ranked show on a Saturday. Consequently, the data cannot be aggregated into anything more than daily, relatively incomparable, snapshots. Delivering this fairly dumb data makes it impossible to estimate larger trends.

At my most cynical, I imagine Netflix intentionally decided to release the most useless data that would be assumed to be important as a way of trolling the industry and its analysts – myself included – who complain endlessly about the lack of available data. Maybe it didn't *deliberately* release the most useless data out of spite, but it is pretty useless nevertheless. Moreover, providing the data is a sleight of hand that appeals to what we assume is important based on the hegemony of linear thinking and occupies our speculation while Netflix digs into data that really matter.

But my biggest hesitation with these lists is that we have no idea how much Netflix viewing is typically represented by these titles, which account for roughly 0.2 per cent of a typical Netflix library. Is it 10 per cent of viewing, 50 per cent, 90 per cent? The 'meaning' of the number varies considerably based on the answer.

Also, Top 10 may be an important metric for ad-supported television, but its importance for a subscriber-funded service is unclear. In linear ad-supported television, 'most watched' probably coincides with the highest advertising revenue, but subscriber-funded services don't benefit as directly from such hits. 'Most watched' is important to Netflix's internal evaluation of its programming expenditures. Expensive shows likely warrant higher viewership to return the investment. Yet, number of viewers isn't the only important factor in even that measure.

Unlike with ad-supported video, the number of viewers needs to be considered in combination with something like a 'satisfaction coefficient' – a value that indicates how important access to the title is to a viewer in deciding to maintain the service. The satisfaction coefficient explains how shows with a small but passionate following derive their value and can be just as, if not more, valuable than 'most watched' shows despite far fewer viewers. In other words, you may be among the millions who watched *Stranger Things*, but Netflix's commissioned romantic comedies might be the thing that really keeps you subscribing. This 'satisfaction coefficient' I'm imagining is data-based but inferred by some behaviour (speed of consumption; immediacy of consumption) and notably feasible at scale only because of the behaviour data available to Netflix. Titles with narrow but passionate support are more sustainable in subscriber funding than many other revenue models that are less able to monetize passion levels – especially with Netflix's scale and ability to conglomerate varied sensibilities. *Media economists have explained that the most mass hits are often less satisfying to consumers than those that are able to service more specific tastes.*[11] Another meaningful metric indicating subscriber satisfaction with the service is how many hours are being streamed. These features operate for all SVODs; however, at this point, only Netflix seems to actively curate a library strategy specific to its industrial conditions.

Of course Netflix wants a lot of people to watch expensive content aimed at attracting a broad audience ('blockbusters'), and it supports those titles through marketing and promotion beyond the interface. But the purpose of these titles is also to generate buzz, unpaid promotion, and cultural discussion that make people who don't subscribe feel left out or that they need to join and see what is going on. These big titles drive word of mouth and generate tons of free promotion, but I'm wary of assuming they play an outsized role in driving people to maintain their subscription. Many of the titles among the most watched are the least different from the programmes you can find on linear television channels and in movie theatres. That suggests such titles were designed to appeal broadly – and they might among Netflix subscribers – but that doesn't mean they play an enormous role in compelling subscribers to continue to pay a monthly fee.

Watching the lists for clues about Netflix may not be useless but requires a good bit of caution. Such analysis is most helpful in revealing new questions and ways of thinking about what the service is doing, or for what it suggests about viewers' desires that aren't being met, rather than for providing any specific wisdom. Watching one country's list over time may begin to reveal patterns, and even more patterns emerge once trends in different lists start to become clear. The trick is remembering that this is actually just a small part of the overall Netflix content strategy.

Comparing lists reveals the different role Netflix might be playing in different places. It is interesting to pivot across lists aggregated at FlixPatrol and see the commonalities and differences between countries. There is certainly evidence of a multinational viewing culture emerging around particular titles, but it is difficult to know the extent of this phenomenon. These lists are also helpful for casual hints – testing is too strong a word – about general questions, such as how strong country of origin may be in driving viewing. Whether new local content shows up in a given country's list is also an important indicator, especially since the most watched lists appear to be influenced considerably by proximity of release. The general mix of national origin for most watched titles is another notable factor. But we have no idea how representative these lists are for all the viewing in a country on a given day. It is easy to base theories on them, but they might illustrate entirely different features than are true of all viewing.

Developing series with the aim of their being the most watched is *part* of Netflix's library strategy; the mistake is assuming this is the whole, or even the primary, strategy. The affordances of SVOD allow Netflix to engage simultaneously in contradictory strategies at the level of title development, which leads to a multifaceted library. Replicating 'mass-targeted' content is among its strategies, but it might be its least consequential. This is why comparisons between Netflix's audience numbers and box-office totals or linear channel viewers are so pointless; there are different business models behind them, so different metrics matter.

One thing to expect is continued change. Although Netflix's repeated pivots in library strategy have mostly been self-determined to this point, future shifts may require responses that result from the adjustments to the broader ecosystem that it has inspired. The next chapter explores how Netflix's peculiar industrial characteristics drive it to prioritize distinctive content.

9
Netflix Content Strategies

Netflix doesn't have a single content strategy. Mostly, the service seeks titles subtly distinct from those typical of linear ad-supported services and titles in alignment with underserved taste clusters. But the industrial dynamic of selling access to a bundle also leads it to do precisely the opposite. Some of its titles are quite consistent with Hollywood blockbuster content so that the blend of strategies appears contradictory and perhaps ill-advised. Netflix's content strategy functions as a sort of Rorschach prompt: most viewers see only the bit of the library that interests them, and thus that corner becomes the totality of their imagined 'Netflix'. It is crucial to forget the hegemony of linear ad-supported services and their demographic focus if seeking to make sense of Netflix's approach. The basic conditions of its venture are that *Netflix needs content viewers desire so much they are willing to pay for it*, and, because it sells access in a bundle, *titles can be successful without being most watched*.

What, if anything, can be said generally about 'Netflix's content' given its efforts to conglomerate and service viewers as a collection of taste communities? Netflix seeks first for its library to be different from what is familiar and readily available on linear ad-supported television, a strategy described here as *shifted 45 degrees*. Its content isn't radically distinct – in fact, it is mostly quite ordinary. But still, it is also subtly and purposively distinctive – often in tone – from the mainstream of commercial linear television.

Part of the difficulty in explaining this – or of making declarative assertions – is that television isn't the same around the globe. Tastes and norms in the US are not the same as in Brazil or Singapore, or even somewhere more culturally proximate such as the UK. What I see as differences in Netflix commissions from US broadcast programmes might seem quite conventional in other countries. Deeply and systematically teasing out these distinctions in order to address precisely where Netflix fits within particular video ecosystems requires a team of researchers familiar with the history and common characteristics of television and film in different countries. I can only really understand Netflix relative to the US market, so that's where I'll focus.

Content shifted 45 degrees aims to describe the way in which most Netflix series commissions don't look like series that I can imagine being commissioned by US linear channels. Though the genres and types of programme content are unremarkable in comparison, their execution is different from what I'd expect from a linear ad-supported channel. Most series are more mature in theme and candour than US series. Not titillating – or titillating for the sake of being titillating (I'm looking at you, HBO) – but not confined to avoiding things perceived to be offensive to 'middle America'. A lot of Netflix series operate with a more European sensibility in terms of sexual frankness. For example, I suspect *Sex Education* does not appear as distinctive to European viewers as it does to me. The same goes for Amazon Prime Video's co-commission *Fleabag*, which would be surprising to find on a US broadcaster but was co-commissioned by BBC Three – then a digital channel, but still the BBC.

Admittedly this distinction from linear television has grown more difficult to establish in the US context as a result of the two decades of series commissioned by cable channels, which significantly shifted the norms of US television established by broadcasters.[1] Many other countries did not experience this substantial intervention in content norms at the start of the century; however, many countries have a longer history of the type of content Jason Mittell terms 'complex' television, which was previously extraordinary in the US context, because their systems involved robust public service broadcasters and cultural policy that prioritized metrics other than attracting the most attention.[2] Cable-commissioned series, from *The Sopranos*, to *Breaking Bad*, to *Mad Men*, and several less famous titles brought significant programming innovation by expanding the types of series available on US television and altered perceptions of content valuable within economies of programme sales. These series that attracted much smaller audiences were supported either entirely by subscriber revenue, as in the case of *The Sopranos* and other HBO series, or by a level of subscriber revenue that enabled the channel to focus on something other than amassing the largest audience. Consequently, the series commissioned by Netflix and some other SVODs are not profoundly differentiated from what some cable channels commission (particularly HBO, Showtime, FX, and AMC) – though they are distinct from what linear ad-supported broadcasters would offer. This is context specific. For example, in Australia, where Netflix subscribers quickly overtook the comparatively few subscribers to the monopoly cable service provider Foxtel, SVOD-commissioned content seemed more distinctive and extraordinary because cable channels had not undertaken similarly innovative commissioning, and a majority of households had never accessed them.

Tone is one of the key tools Netflix uses to achieve its 45-degree shift. Tone accounts for a lot of how Netflix is able to adjust slightly the conventional norms of programmes found on linear ad-supported channels. The types of content are the same, but the differentiation arises from how its commissions tell their stories and the characters that function as the moral centre of those stories. Netflix is a mass commercial service in Australia, Canada, the US, and the UK; its aim is by no means 'art house' (which might mean 'shifted 180 degrees'). Having a different tone often provides the strategically desired distinction for titles in the Netflix library.

Netflix also develops content for verticals largely underserved by linear ad-supported services. A clear example of this is the amount of sci-fi and fantasy in its library. Science fiction – an admittedly broad vertical – has devoted fans but has not been considered a genre capable of attracting an audience sizable enough to encourage linear ad-supported services to commission a lot of this content. But Netflix's ability to aggregate sci-fi fans across national contexts builds a bigger audience and enables it to identify complexity within the category and connect with other adjacent taste clusters. Or consider the extent to which many Netflix-commissioned movies focus on verticals that Hollywood studios have de-emphasized in recent decades, such as romantic comedies and movies about female characters. Or, as noted earlier, many Netflix-commissioned series feature stories about teens and young adults, a target difficult for linear services to reach and often too narrow an audience for focus. Netflix has talked about its 'clean teen' content (perhaps a subvertical within children and family) geared at pre-teens which doesn't simultaneously seek to attract older peers with more adult-themes. The narrow scope of an age-defined audience at a national level often meant adolescent programming had to appeal broadly, but because Netflix serves such an expansive base it is able to programme for pre-teens and teens separately, and increasingly with the range of titles – science fiction, romantic comedy, adventure – typically offered only to adults.

Another aspect of the 45-degree shift is the tonal difference of many series in the Netflix library that otherwise appear as conventional content types. The need for linear broadcasters to construct a mass audience requires taking a 'mass attitude' towards the content they produce. As a result, a lot of linear ad-supported commissions avoid having too strong a viewpoint lest they risk alienating viewers that don't share that sensibility and diminishing the audience. Linear-commissioned programmes might incorporate more unorthodox attitudes through secondary characters as a way to try to make those outside the mainstream feel rudimentarily hailed. Or characters with attributes uncommon for television might be included in comedy series so that their difference can be laughed at to ensure the core mass audience would not find them off-putting.

But Netflix is more likely to put those secondary characters at the centre of its shows.

Exploring Netflix's licensed titles and considering the shows Netflix *doesn't* license also helps reveal a lot about the subtle distinctions of its programming. Many of the top ratings hits in the US have not been included in the Netflix library. This may be a matter of studios demanding licence fees that outweigh the value of the shows, but – and related – it also may be that the features of shows such as *CSI*, *NCIS*, and *Law & Order*, which attracted large audiences on linear ad-supported services, don't offer the differentiation that compels Netflix subscription.

Also, a lot of Netflix series assume viewers watch them in a manner different from content developed for linear television. Because people are less likely to walk into a room and 'turn on Netflix' in the way they use linear television to provide a background, Netflix commissions tend to demand more attention and focus. They also don't need to keep repeating plot details, because viewers are less likely to have 'missed' an episode and more likely to have seen past episodes more recently than a week previously. Many Netflix series are narratively complex and subtle in ways that make them difficult to follow if they are viewed distractedly. Again, such differences are often slight and only apparent when you watch series, not from scrolling title cards on the home screen, but these features lead to storytelling differentiated from linear norms. It is no accident that the basic crime and law procedurals that draw the most American viewers to linear prime time cannot be found in the Netflix library. When Netflix commissions or licenses 'police content', it looks different, as in *Unbelievable*, *Bodyguard*, or *Criminal*.

But, as introduced, there are exceptions – often glaring exceptions. There is arguably a vertical (or verticals) of Netflix content that isn't notably distinctive and which has not shifted 45 degrees at all. A lot of the 'Hollywood-style' movies commissioned, such as *6 Underground, Triple Frontier*, or *Murder Mystery*, are difficult to claim as particularly distinctive, likewise something like *Fuller House*. It is significant that those first three movies – *6 Underground* in particular – were among the most watched titles in many countries around the globe in 2019.[3] That doesn't make them more valuable to Netflix or more 'on brand' than other programmes. But 'Hollywood-style movie' might also be a (sub)vertical. Although subscribing to Netflix isn't going to replace the experience of going to the cinema to see a big blockbuster, the ability to watch this type of movie on a Saturday night probably adds value to the service distinct from how it is appreciated as a source of content suited for more particular sensibilities.

Shifting 45 degrees – except when intentionally not making such a shift – might seem a ridiculous way of describing a content strategy, but it could be the only general claim that is really defensible. The affordances that allow Netflix's content strategies stymie the desire or expectation of understanding its programming as just one thing, or at least as not riddled with contradictions. *If it is one thing, for the most part, it is a focus on characters, stories, and ways of telling stories with a subtle difference from those that dominate the marketplace of linear television and Hollywood blockbusters.*

One of the reasons it is so difficult to make sense of Netflix – beyond the ways it is distinguished by its industrial differences – is its ability to carry out the equivalent of self-counterprogramming. Most of its content is slightly distinctive from the video entertainment available on linear channels; some of it is clearly trying to be very much like Hollywood fare, but this too is made distinctive because of the *experience* through which it is offered by Netflix. Although our personal sensibilities may lead us to gravitate towards an array of preferred taste clusters, we are also whimsical creatures who don't always want exactly the same thing. Also, many subscribers are part of households, and what we watch together often differs from what we choose to watch when alone. A key advantage of a bundled offering with on-demand delivery is the ability for Netflix and other SVODs to service the different tastes of individuals in a household and to also offer them an easy way to watch something together.

Netflix doesn't have *a* content strategy and there isn't a quintessentially Netflix series or movie. Instead, I could point to many that enact different and particular strategies that are valuable precisely for their differentiation: the Hollywood-style movie; the angsty young adult drama; the raunchy mom-com; the buzzy-Emmy bait title; or the richly place-based genre story such as *Kingdom*. The genius of Netflix's system is its ability to be all these things.

Content strategy in practice: considering One Day at a Time

The strategy of offering varied content to help viewers with different sensibilities feel in distinct ways, and the relation of that strategy to existing scheduling and development strategies for other video industries, may make more sense if grounded in an extended example that might also illustrate how strategies for targeting sensibilities aren't entirely separate from targeting demographics. To put it in applied terms, how is the fact that I like mom-coms and complicated political thrillers such as *Borgen* and *Madam Secretary* not just about the fact that I'm a highly educated, straight, white, American woman of a certain age?

Demographic factors aren't absent from this calculus; they can play a role, but not *the* role played, in linear ad-supported strategy. First, particular demographic features are not being sold as they are in an ad-funded context. For SVODs, demographic characteristics may align with particular taste communities in a way that becomes a shorthand for a sensibility, but sensibility is neither determined by nor exclusive to those with the demographic feature. For example, LGBTQ subscribers may be more likely to watch programmes with LGBTQ characters, but that is probably only one component of a sensibility. Viewers who like shows with central gay characters may be a taste community (though not one to which all gay people belong and also one which includes people who aren't gay), but this is still a pretty blunt level of potential connection. Netflix layers that sensibility on top of others – consider how the co-CEO Ted Sarandos talks about *One Day at a Time* to Joe Adalian: 'The unique value that it serves ... is that there were five or six different viewer groups who have a very strong affinity for that show. Latino for sure, LGBT for sure, female for sure. And it tells a different story than is being told on Netflix.'[4] Sarandos's comments blur terminology (here 'viewer groups' are probably 'taste communities'). 'Latino' or 'LGBT' aren't known demographic features of subscribers. Rather, they identify viewers – or, more precisely, viewer profiles

– that have established a consumption pattern that includes Latino or LGBT characters. In the case of *One Day at a Time*, the series services viewers who have a pattern of viewing such content as well as those interested in 'feel-good' and 'goofy' family comedies – per its official Netflix tone designators.

As Adalian reports, quoting Netflix VP of product Todd Yellin, 'Nowadays, in our modern world, hit play once and it tells us volumes more than knowing you're a 31-year-old woman or a 72-year-old man or a 19-year-old guy.' Or, quoting Sarandos, 'It's just as likely that a 75-year-old man in Denmark likes *Riverdale* as my teenage kids.' Or Yellin again, 'We find [demographics] to be greater and greater nonsense, and we are disproving it every day.' These claims may be hyperbolic, but the underlying point remains valid. We have learned to think about demographic features such as age and gender because they have been identifiable in the audience research conducted for linear television services. Market research conducted by studios or channels has not sought to map preferences and sensibilities through actual viewing of a range of different content in the manner of Netflix, and it was largely impossible until recently. Such demographic features tell us something about likely preferences and sensibility, but profiles of actual viewing tell us much more. And the truth is that Netflix does not know whether the man in Denmark that likes *Riverdale* is seventy-five, just that the rest of his viewing appears consistent with that of an older viewer.

One Day at a Time provides a good illustration of all the concepts merged together. It is a family comedy (vertical), which is a type of programme found far more commonly on linear ad-supported television than

Netflix. As such, it could have aired on a US ad-supported network, but the need to attract a mass audience would have made that network uncertain about its story about a Cuban-American family and a teen girl recognizing her lesbian identity. Although those features may attract viewers with a pattern of watching shows with Latino and LGBT characters, in seeking a mass audience, an ad-supported outlet would be more concerned about those who might not watch on account of those features. But Netflix can disregard creative decisions necessary to aggregate a general mass audience; instead it probably identified the series as a title that services viewers interested in stories about Latinos and LGBT characters, and who don't care if family stories are set in something other than US television's heteronormative, upper-middle-class, white norms.

The tonal features of feel-good and goofy further distinguish the series within this category of family comedy. These are apt tonal descriptors that identify how the series is not cloyingly saccharine – which is often the case of tonally 'heartfelt' US family comedies designed to construct a mass audience. The specific blend identifies how *One Day at a Time* strikes a tone that validates the importance of family while also presenting it with all its complex dynamics and relationships. I'd describe the series as most similar to *The Cosby Show* in its tone (albeit now a very complicated title). Many might misread this comparison as being about the non-white ethnicity of the families in both (a demographic category), but that is not a vector. *The Cosby Show* too is feel-good and goofy. I'd use different words to describe other US network-family comedies, such as *Roseanne* or *Home Improvement*, that derived their humour in other ways.

One Day at a Time is also an interesting example because it is a series that many television journalists and fans were disappointed to see limited to three seasons (on Netflix). In ending its commission, Netflix wasn't suggesting it was a bad show, or that its viewers were unimportant, just that it wasn't achieving what had been expected in attracting audiences across taste clusters to add an amount of value to its library proportionate to its production cost. That problem might have been more a function of Netflix than the series, as Netflix isn't a place immediately considered for family comedy. Nor was it included in its library available to 'kids' profiles. Subscriber-funded services still need programmes to achieve certain metrics, but we shouldn't apply linear norms of success – such as the creation of hundreds of episodes – as a standard measure.

There are two other revealing insights in Sarandos's description of *One Day at a Time*. His description of 'different viewer groups who have a very strong affinity' is a notable phrase. It hints at the existence of *a scale of affinity*, or that Netflix isn't weighting all viewership equally but has some way to measure a 'satisfaction coefficient' that addresses the different value people place on what they view. For example, I may have watched *6 Underground* because it was a fun Friday night movie, but watching *One Day at a Time* with my family was worth a year's subscription to Netflix. I'm not sure how my viewing data might indicate this value, but it would be a significant advancement for the intelligence of the service if it could. Also, Sarandos's comment that 'it tells a different story than is being told on Netflix' supports the assertion that its library strategy is multifaceted and designed to aggregate satisfaction by serving different needs.

This analysis requires a bit of speculation, but even speculative understandings help reveal how the thinking behind SVOD library and content strategies both connects with and differs from strategy typical of theatrical film or linear ad-supported television. It is a nuanced business, and nuance is lost in sweeping statements such as 'SVODs only make three seasons' or 'Netflix started cancelling everything.' Those on the outside trying to make sense of these practices aren't far behind those on the inside still in the processes of trial and error. Understanding SVODs does not require entirely new ways of thinking, but it does require us not to assume that all the things we know from previous video businesses apply or apply in the same ways.

10
Netflix's Approach to Being Global

What and where is Netflix? Or, to what extent can we consider Netflix as a single, global entity? Can we speak of 'Netflix', or should we speak with modification of the many Netflixes – for example, of Netflix Australia, Netflix Belgium, etc.? This is an important question, because the company's approach – at least since the start of the Netflix 3.0 phase – challenges the domestic/foreign dichotomy that has long organized thinking about video and video services.

A good starting point is appreciating how the 'reels' of Netflix's structuring characteristics line up to encourage a specific strategy in the global market. As noted above, as a pure play service with a general library that is transitioning from licensed to bespoke ownership, Netflix has ventured on its global expansion differently from Hollywood's typical approach to 'foreign' markets. From very early on in its efforts to expand its subscriber base beyond North America, Netflix began commissioning content from the markets it sought to serve (see figure 2, p. 93). The service then shared those commissions with its many libraries, adding a counterflow to the typical, one-way content movement out of the US. The fact that only roughly 40 per cent of titles in Netflix libraries – even the US library – are US productions weakens assertions of commonality among 'American' streamers and of casually identifying Netflix as American beyond its ownership (see figure 4).

Figure 4   Percentage of US-produced titles in twelve Netflix national libraries

This figure illustrates the general consistency in the amount of US-produced content across twelve major libraries, as well as those with slightly more or less than average.

161

Netflix offers significant evidence of its aim to be a cosmopolitan service – an admittedly tricky term – that disrupts the foregrounding of national identity that has been key to constructing video audiences to date. From a critical perspective, there are many reasons to be suspicious or wary of this cosmopolitanism, but the company's eschewal of typical Hollywood strategy also requires good faith engagement with deviation from practices considered characteristic of cultural imperialism and globalization in the media studies literature.[1] It is reasonable to expect Netflix's strategy has both benefits and limitations relative to long-standing critical debates about Hollywood norms, and a small scale study has found a significant increase among foreign content viewing among a sample of US subscribers.[2] Among key considerations are that it remains one SVOD among many and that SVODs exist as one video source among several. This multiplicity provides much greater ecosystem diversity than was typical when past thinking on these dynamics developed.

Is Netflix the 'same' everywhere?

One way to ground Netflix geographically and assess the similarity of its offerings is through its specific libraries of content. Data about library holdings aren't ideal information. Libraries only tell us what is available, not what is watched. Patterns across libraries – as in the analysis in chapter 8 – reveal insight into broader corporate strategy, and change in these patterns over time might hint at aspects of success and failure in terms of what compels subscribers. Similarly, the limited 'most watched' title data provides daily snapshots of what is watched in different places, although, as noted, this is likely a narrow indication of content viewed and valued.

Notably, it is not just the Netflix libraries that vary. Understanding Netflix's role in any given territory requires appreciating the historical and cultural norms regarding audiovisual content, the further options offered by internet and other distribution technologies, the formal and informal regulations that structure the storytelling of these technologies, and the availability and affordability of both internet access and the technologies used to engage with video content. The availability of Netflix in a great many places in no way suggests it is or 'means' the 'same' across those borders.

Netflix is differentiated across territories – not only in its library but also in its business strategy. For example, it has created special pricing for mobile phone-only access in India in response to the conditions there and experimented with a linear 'channel' in France. Such variation in business model requires careful acknowledgement of Netflix's differentiation in analysis, such as noting that it may be nationally varied with regard to more than its content offering.

Based on the limited data available – such as library analysis, the daily Top 10 lists, and annual data that is released highlighting most watched content in different territories – Netflix is both globally consistent in its offerings yet distinctive in geographic, cultural, and linguistic clusters at the national level. More than half – 60 per cent – of the Netflix library is available across its territories, which accounts for the commonality. Another roughly 20 per cent commonality can be seen in clusters within Latin America, in Europe (excluding the UK), and among the English-language dominant

'Anglosphere' plus India.[3] Major Asian countries such as Japan and South Korea have less regional similarity and instead show greater national variation, which is enabled by uncommonly high levels of domestic content. In other work, I identified this as the distinction between Netflix's consistent and variable markets.[4] Notably, Netflix is most variable in Asia, which is also the region with the lowest penetration. This thesis that conceives of both globalizing and cluster/nation specificity needs continued monitoring, given that countries exhibiting some of the greatest variation are among those with lower global SVOD penetration.

Again, an important attribute of Netflix's library is that the consistency results from significant multinational sourcing. The evidence to date suggests its experiment of providing a video service that is sourced from multiple territories is a viable and distinctive strategy – though certainly far from the only one. An important part of why this works is the subscriber funding and on-demand access. A linear ad-funded global service would have very different priorities.

This analysis remains admittedly limited. Meaningful analysis requires deeper data about viewing behaviour to really appreciate what is happening and to evaluate the cultural implications. We can divine bits from the structure – for example, in addition to not being the same everywhere, a commercial service is not going to treat all markets in the same way. Territories with more subscribers are likely to receive more commissioning unless the pattern of viewing suggests that users in the country appreciate Netflix for its access to content produced elsewhere. For example, in 2020, Australia had the highest penetration of Netflix subscription, although, as a smaller country, that meant only about

6 million subscribers. Compared with other highly subscribed countries, Netflix commissioned comparatively little Australian content. Australia's high adoption is probably because of its relatively low adoption of cable or satellite, which, in turn, results from the lack of a service with a strong value proposition. Thus, Australians may regard Netflix as worth paying for because it provides access to content created in the US and elsewhere generally unavailable across its roughly sixteen broadcast channels. Or, given the heavy reliance on broadcast and low penetration of technologies such as digital video recorders, a lot of the value may result from the on-demand experience Netflix offers. But the point is that, just because Netflix is available in 190 countries, and has produced content in forty-one, doesn't mean that all of those territories will ever be the source of commissioned content or that there is likely to be anything like equity among those that do.

As of 2022, Netflix's US origin remains strongly imprinted on the service, but it may not remain so. Figure 5 illustrates how the percentage of Netflix's commissions have shifted as the service has become more global in its subscriber base. Additionally, as the broader dynamics of international video trade adjust in response to content conglomerates pivoting from licensing their content to national channels to offering direct-to-consumer SVODs, the content available for licensing will change. Moreover, Netflix's strategy will adjust to pending shifts in the competitive marketplaces of countries that provide a significant amount of its revenue. The adoption of these services, both in the US and globally, will also lead to adjustments in strategy.

Netflix isn't the same everywhere. That is clear. But how and why are other questions entirely. There are

Figure 5 Percentage of Netflix US commissions to all commissions, 2015–2020

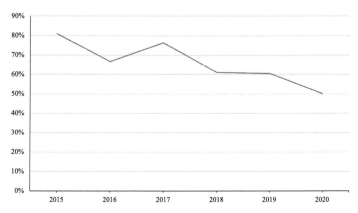

This figure depicts the steady decline in the percentage of US-produced Netflix commissions as the service has expanded its subscriber base outside the US.

common features, but what Netflix means – how it is experienced and understood by people using it – depends considerably on national context. It functions as a mass-market service in very few countries, and that dynamic is likely to persist. Examining *how* Netflix is multinational, and using fresh eyes to investigate what content strategies it is able to use in advancing its multinational reach instead of applying ideas based on how video services have been 'global' in the past, may aid the building of more relevant theories about how and why video connects with different audiences regardless of their nation of residence. We should be aware of, but not expect, the same dynamics as have been revealed in decades of multinational programme trade and transnational satellite channels.

166

Netflix's Approach to Being Global

Why do people subscribe to a service that mostly offers foreign content?

Even in the US, national Netflix libraries offer more titles foreign to the country than created within it. The idea that people outside the US willingly subscribe to Netflix for access to content that is largely foreign, though mostly from the US, verges on the heretical in some circles. But looking at the level of service adoption and library composition, and acknowledging the minimal available data about what is actually watched, this seems to be the case. This reality by no means negates findings developed throughout the twentieth century about audience preferences for 'proximate' content – I don't contest a general preference for 'local'. Rather, this is another instance in which we have to set aside assumptions based on how other mechanisms of multi-territory video distribution have worked and start from the different underlying foundation of SVOD services.

There are three possible explanations for Netflix's popularity despite the lack of locally produced titles: *Netflix offers titles proximate or meaningful in other ways*; *Netflix offers a better experience for watching US titles already pervasive on linear services*; and *Netflix offers US titles that are different from those linear importers have prioritized.*

In many ways, the obvious extent to which Netflix subscribers do not sign up for 'local' content is validation of the argument about the importance of experience and an illustration of how Netflix is a complement or supplement to existing local audiovisual services rather than a competitor to or replacement for them. Looking at Netflix libraries around the world, it seems unlikely

167

that access to local titles drives subscription. While it may initially motivate some, the local content on offer is rarely enough to sustain those viewers. In many cases, it probably results from government pressure or regulatory action rather than market forces.

In Australia in 2019, Lobato and Scarlata found the Australian library featured only 1.7 per cent of Australian content, composed of seventeen movies, forty-three licensed series, six series commissions, three stand-up comedy specials, and thirteen documentaries. It is very difficult to believe that the roughly half of Australian households who willingly pay for Netflix monthly do so because local content is a priority when this is the case.[5] Notably, Lobato and Scarlata found there were more Australian series in the US library than in the Australian library.

So why do people subscribe? Perhaps because other types of proximity – the idea that people like things that are familiar – are also important. Netflix's industrial characteristics of subscriber funding, on-demand access, and ability to service tastes and sensibilities too small to be valuable to channels aimed at aggregating a sizable national audience enable it to address those proximities. It may be the case that audiences prefer distinctive as much as local content, or that they appreciate having what Netflix offers as an alternative (Netflix is a complement). During a 2021 investor call, Netflix executives noted that the service accounted for only 10 per cent of viewing in the United States, data affirmed by Nielsen.[6] This suggests that the service's role in the marketplace is far from outsized, although it is unclear how this figure compares to its use in other countries; certainly, it is much lower in the majority of countries in which Netflix operates as a niche service.

The idea that proximity is more complicated than a preference for content that represents one's geographic location is not new. More recent writing by scholars such as Joseph Straubhaar and Antonio C. La Pastina has addressed how proximate 'genres, themes, and values' also drive viewers.[7] But such attributes were difficult to study systematically because detailed audience research is needed to answer questions about why viewers prefer titles, and viewers themselves often have difficulty explaining their tastes. Foreign programme sales were based on titles likely to attract the biggest mass audience within the nation or channel's reach, and, as a result, the most widely shared preferences were prioritized. Until SVODs, foreign programme sales operated entirely within the hegemonies of linear and demographic thinking. Moreover, distinctive content, or content that provides a variety of tonal qualities and is geared to serving audiences smaller than are likely to be attractive to a linear ad-supported service, hasn't been made available in the past, so we've never had much of a way to assess it. The data Netflix collects can't explain tastes, but it can identify viewing behaviour and patterns among texts at an unprecedented scale from which the service can develop ideas about what compels viewing.

One taste cluster – and corresponding taste community – where non-geographic proximity is clearly prioritized is among titles about young adults. For teen viewers, interest in stories about being a teen seems to be a much stronger aspect of identity than the proximity of local reference. Whether the transnational success of titles such as *13 Reasons Why* or the extent to which Netflix has pioneered a subgenre of teen romantic comedies (designed for teens, not adults working through teen glories and traumas), this is clearly an audience under-served by linear ad-supported channels and one difficult for them to serve because they don't account for that much 'attention' as an audience segment, and little that suits them suits older or younger viewers. Netflix has commissioned content about teens in multiple countries: *Baby* (Italy), *Elite* (Spain), *Sex Education, Free Reign* (UK), *On My Block* (US); also *Tall Girl* (US) ranked among France's 2019 Top 10 titles, and *Never Have I Ever* (US) was the most streamed show in India and Brazil and in the Top 10 of a country on every continent when it dropped.

There are other sensibilities that remain unserved or underserved in the linear ad-supported market that Netflix can build into a viable taste community. The tonal distinctions discussed in chapter 9 suggest other ways by which Netflix serves sensibilities that may be stronger drivers of viewing than geographic, cultural, or linguistic proximity.

Within the emerging SVOD lore there are also some cases that may more directly contradict the prioriti-zation of local content. For instance, Netflix CEO Reed Hastings disclosed that the Swedish commissioned series *Quicksand* was viewed fifteen times more in the rest of the world than in Sweden and was particularly widely seen in Argentina.[8] This is understandable – well, not the popularity in Argentina; *Quicksand* isn't particularly Swedish or about Sweden. Its story about destructive teen relationships and violence resonates, unfortunately, fairly universally. It is also worth recog-nizing this as an indication of the scale of information Netflix possesses about the extent to which people watch 'foreign' and non-US content when it is recom-mended to them. Another Netflix-supplied datapoint comes from Diego Avalos, Vice President for Original Content for Spain and Latin America, who disclosed that 50 per cent of subscribing households have watched content neither in English nor in their native language.[9] 'Have watched' is a pretty low bar, but it is also notable, especially given the pre-Netflix lore about the refusal of US audiences to read subtitles or accept dubbing.

There are other 'data anecdotes' – 90 per cent of viewing of the German drama *Dark* was outside Germany; 75 per cent of Turkish content viewing comes from outside Turkey; more than 90 per cent of views of Israeli content have come from outside Israel.[10] Without context, these bits of data don't reveal a lot. Given the global dispersion of viewers, most subscribers are outside the nation producing any particular title, and for every *Dark* there may be a domestic production for which 90 per cent of viewing is from the country that created it. The multifaceted strategy of the service encourages its commissioning and licensing of different types of content that likely perform in widely variable ways. The point here is simply that the peculiar characteristics of global SVODs also might allow for different dynamics than have been observed and theorized in media studies scholarship and industry lore to date.

A second reason why subscribers in many countries pay for a service that offers mostly foreign content is because it provides a better way to watch a lot of the material that already fills the schedules of many domestic linear ad-supported channels. Netflix and other owned-IP SVODs may offer access to these same shows but make it easier to watch them by giving viewers access whenever they want and without ads. And there may be other experiential aspects: a German subscriber may choose to watch *The Good Place* on Netflix instead of on a German linear channel because of the value provided by the experience, and maybe other factors, such as a preference to watch in English instead of having it dubbed.

Looking through the non-Netflix-commissioned US-produced titles that ranked in the Australian Top 10 lists in a recent month revealed the popularity of *Brooklyn Nine-Nine*, *Riverdale*, *The Blacklist*, and *Community*. Of these, only *The Blacklist* was a strong 'hit' by US commercial standards. *Riverdale* is the only one of these series exclusive to Netflix in Australia; one season of *Brooklyn Nine-Nine* and *The Blacklist* are available from other services, and *Community* is fully available on Stan (domestic SVOD) and Amazon Prime Video, and two seasons are on ABC iView (publicly funded, commercial-free VOD). There's not a lot on which to base an argument here – the most watched list gives me little insight into what other titles Australians are viewing – but the fact that these titles achieved daily Top 10 status over multiple days, *despite being available on linear and other domestic SVODs and AVODs*, suggests support for the idea that non-US viewers appreciate the experience offered by Netflix to watch series available to them through linear services.

Moreover, Netflix may be *offering different US content*, particularly that unlikely to be purchased by foreign linear ad-supported channels, because it is considered too niche or unlikely to attract a mass audience. Again, to really appreciate these dynamics, we need experts on local libraries and other local services to evaluate the value proposition Netflix offers in different countries.

So a final reason why Netflix's foreign content may be attractive is that its ability to identify and develop for taste clusters leads it to license content unlikely to have been licensed by services seeking to attract mass attention. Particularly in the US, the characteristics of content developed for cable channels throughout the 2000s have been too specific in their sensibility to be attractive to channels seeking a large audience. Such titles may have been offered by cable/satellite services that have economics based in some level of subscriber payment.

The subscribers Netflix attracts from outside the US aren't those who have known only locally produced content. Exported content has been ubiquitous in many screen cultures around the globe. But Netflix offers a superior experience of that 'foreign' content – and content that is of equivalent quality and often a little bit different from what is already available. For those who make the choice to subscribe, that 'difference' is a valued attribute.

The likely reality that most Netflix viewing is not of local titles – at least outside the US and perhaps in variable markets – isn't an indication that people don't care about whether or not content is local. Rather, the lesson is understanding that a desire for geographically proximate content is just one thing that motivates viewing interest. Most viewers have access to linear channels that provide local content – often for free – and if the data point of Netflix occupying only 10 per cent of viewing time is more broadly true, it is not attracting an exceptional amount of viewing time. I can't imagine there are many Netflix subscribers who watch only Netflix; most also view a significant amount of local linear ad- or publicly funded programming as well. Given such choice, the selection of Netflix doesn't indicate a lack of desire for the options otherwise available; rather, it shows that it is valued as a supplement.

How is Netflix's content multinational?

Netflix's general approach to its commissions – US and otherwise – has often seemed somewhat counterintuitive, but of course that 'intuition' has been built from linear norms, demographic thinking, and foreign sales of programmes to channels, not to individual subscribers. This last point is particularly important in relation to content strategy. *The niches and submarkets targeted by linear services when acquiring foreign content are limited to those that are significant within a national pool of potential viewers.* Netflix can aggregate sensibilities beyond national boundaries, which is a crucial part of how it is able to differentiate its own offerings from those of linear ad-funded channels.

Notably, many of Netflix's series don't seem like shows designed for viewers spread across the world – at least what we've come to expect as characteristic of such shows. Hollywood blockbuster movies are a good example of conventional internationalizing strategy: they tell stories without local specificity that don't rely on dialogue and are mostly spectacle and action. But, in contrast, a lot of Netflix commissions tend to be very grounded in particular places. Netflix VP of Development Kelly Luegenbiehl captures this well in describing Netflix's strategy: 'When we see that great local impact and the really authentic and specific stories, that's where they're finding the more universal, global audience. So the more local that we are and the more specific we are, the more universal we actually

174

are.'[11] Netflix executives say things like this a lot, and saying it doesn't make it so. But, to some extent, these claims are supported by the service's commissioning.

This strategy seems the opposite of what has typically been expected of internationalization that has attempted to tell 'universal' stories – often devoid of cultural specificity – to achieve audience scale. Decades of research indicating that people prefer local content or content 'proximate' to that familiar has led to strategies that try to balance a desire for local specificity with that universal scale. This is a tricky endeavour. Co-productions across Europe that mix signifiers of different countries and cultures into an unrecognizable 'Europe' have been described as 'Europudding' and heavily critiqued. A similar strategy is to make content 'placeless' by eliminating geographic specificity so that people might assume the story is 'local'; this is a strategy typical of many titles set in a nondescript, urban cosmopolitan spaces. But Luegenbiehl describes the opposite of this – that Netflix achieves transnational interest by telling stories clearly set in different places.

Of course Luegenbiehl isn't describing the Netflix library in its entirety; contradiction is both characteristic and strategic. Some verticals use conventional tools of internationalization. What might be seen as Netflix's 'Hollywood-style' vertical illustrates this by aiming broadly with action and spectacle and using locations and talent from around the globe in a manner very similar to what has become the conventional 'internationalizing' Hollywood strategy (6 *Underground*, *Extraction*, *Murder Mystery*, *Triple Frontier*, *Sense8*). But there is a contrasting group of Netflix commissions that are set in particular places and times (*Kingdom*, *Money Heist*, *Narcos*, *Tiger King*, *The Crown*) and probably many others that don't turn up at the very top of 'most viewed' lists yet still add considerable value to the service.

As the 'Hollywood-style' vertical indicates, the intentional contradictions quickly grow tricky and make 'but what about?' arguments easy picking. To examine the multiple ways that local specificity can be integrated into commissions, let's consider a specific place that I can talk about somewhat intelligently: Australia. To be clear, my premise here is that local specificity is one of several attributes Netflix seeks in its commissions, and that *local specificity is important mostly because of the attributes it brings to the storytelling, not because people in a specific country are particularly driven to subscribe to Netflix to see stories set in that country.*

Among Netflix's Australian commissions, co-commissions and licensed titles, I can see a couple of different strategies. Netflix made a big swing in commissioning a series called *Tidelands*. Unfortunately, it was an ambitious effort and a miss by most accounts. *Tidelands* blends drug thriller with supernatural soap in its story about tension in a small coastal town between human drug dealers and the part human, part siren 'Tidelanders' who help them. It looks as if the series had a sizable budget, and it was clearly set in Australia, though the characters weren't particularly Australian, and neither were several of the main cast. In my expert opinion, *Tidelands* was not a good a show – not because of its Australianness or lack of it – it just didn't work. It blended too many tones and genres in a way that made it emotionally unintelligible. But it is characteristic of one of Netflix's local strategies, which is to spend considerably on a title very clearly placed somewhere specific with a story that also services a vertical.[12] *Kingdom* in South Korea is a more successful example.

Netflix has also co-commissioned three series with the public-service Australian Broadcasting Corporation: *Pine Gap*, *Glitch*, and *The Letdown*. *Pine Gap* and *Glitch* are probably a second-tier budget commitment in comparison with *Tidelands*, *The Letdown* even less. *Pine Gap* is a pretty straightforward espionage thriller set in a joint US–Australian intelligence facility. A lot of the story is about the contentious relationship between the Americans and Australians and their negotiation of a threat to their diplomacy from China. *Pine Gap* has recognizably Australian features while still being very accessible to non-Australians, especially Americans. In some ways, it might look like the ideal series for a multi-territory service, but, in reality, the fact that it was a pretty conventional espionage thriller – arguably not shifted 45 degrees – may have limited its contribution to the library. Netflix also commissioned the second season of a comparable series called *Secret City* that was originally commissioned by the cable service Foxtel. *Secret City* is stronger and a more complex thriller. It also features a 'strong female lead' – a consistent differentiating feature of Netflix commissions – which is a notable shift from its literary source material. *Secret City* is arguably more Australian (*Pine Gap* being so isolated in the artificial context of a military base), and the complex relationship of the country with the American and Chinese governments figures prominently here as well. *Secret City* is probably what Netflix hoped for in commissioning *Pine Gap*. Both are clearly 'placed' in Australia but offer limited cultural specificity.

Glitch and *The Letdown* are very different, as is the pure commission *Lunatics*. These series are identifiable to Australians as featuring Australian actors in Australian settings, but they aren't profoundly or generally about Australia. They are probably more indicative of everyday Australian culture (minus *Glitch*'s story of people coming back from the dead) than *Secret City* and *Pine Gap*, which wear their Australianness in the depiction of official Australian institutions. *The Letdown* and *Lunatics* fit the 45-degree shift strategy. (*The Letdown* was an ABC co-commission, though it probably wouldn't have been commissioned by a commercial channel because of its tone.)

Finally, the licensed titles. *Wanted* is an exclusive and among those rumoured to have done particularly well on Netflix. It is a series about two women fugitives, an on-the-run thriller through some of Australia's most distinctive scenery. It is not really *about* Australia, not really even about everyday Australian life. The library also includes some of the most recognizable series Australia has produced, such as *Please Like Me* and *Kath and Kim*. As a newcomer to Australia, I have more difficulty appreciating what these shows signify amid the broader library of titles Netflix could have purchased. Reflecting instead on the question of what titles are licensed from the US, I would argue that the service's selections tend (with some exceptions) not to be broad hits but, rather, those aligned with a taste cluster strategy.

The point here is that the local commissioning and licensing strategy may seem all over the place if you are thinking in terms of the past hegemonies that led to the expectation of a singular strategy aimed at attracting the most attention. But if you think in terms of aggregating underserved sensibilities and tones applicable to viewers in many countries who are looking for something a little different – and allow that there is significant variation in budget and corresponding viewership expectations – the difference among the titles begins to make more sense, even if it also remains difficult to draw strong conclusions. This is a very small amount of evidence, but it doesn't suggest a priority on 'universal' subject matter, and these series are Australian in very different ways. At this point, there isn't evidence that any one of these strategies is a priority.

The key questions I'd like people with expertise in other markets to investigate are whether Netflix commissions are like or different from what one might expect to find on linear ad-supported channels, and, if so, how? The same question goes for publicly funded public service broadcasters. Then, to consider how the series are 'of the country' – what I describe very briefly here as how they are Australian. Do they have features of cultural specificity that would prevent relocating the story somewhere else? Or could the story be produced elsewhere with minor alteration? I would expect there to be considerable variation – the ability to conglomerate niches would support that. Deeper analysis of patterns will be helpful in gauging to what extent Netflix is doing something different with its strategy for attracting a multi-territory audience and what the implications might be, especially if patterns grow clearer with deeper local library development and expert analysis that can identify cross-market trends.

Why does Netflix commission content from many places?

Why would Netflix commission programming from around the globe? When I first identified the scale of its multi-territory commissioning – that over half of adult series commissions were from outside the US by

2020 – I initially assumed this was a strategy to drive subscriptions in those countries. This may be part of the strategy, but likely not precisely in the way I first speculated. For example, it is difficult to believe that the addition of Australian titles in the library produced a clear uptick in Australian subscribers. Some new subscribers may have come in with the launch of particularly high profile or buzzy local content. For instance, *Lunatics* received a lot of coverage – much of which was fairly negative – but it successfully broke through the clutter of entertainment enough to register in awareness.[13] People who wanted to understand the phenomenon would have to subscribe to Netflix to find out what was being talked about. But I suspect a buzzy, non-Australian series such as *The Crown* would have a fairly equivalent effect.

To be clear, I am not suggesting that local content produces no effect on driving subscriptions, just that it probably isn't as strong a driver as many assume. And, as a result, the strategic value of local content is limited, and that might deter it from featuring much cultural specificity. Netflix likely accrues perceived value and positive brand awareness when it commissions local content even if the national origin of that content isn't all that important to subscribers. Producing an expensive show such as *Tidelands* – which at times is basically an advertisement for Australian beach vacations – might make Australian subscribers feel valued even if the show doesn't really fit their taste or sensibility. People know Netflix is a global service, and it is culturally affirming to be contributing to the global library.

Also, local commissioning is good business in multiple ways, even though it may not be a subscriber's primary driver; Netflix's brand reputation is tied to a kind of cosmopolitan capital that is strengthened by widely sourced commissions. Furthermore, local commissions both help Netflix stay out of local regulators' sights and assist in supporting local production sectors and thus building goodwill. The European Union moved early to subject Netflix to local content quotas that are applied to linear channels – in a manner I'd argue is ill-considered due to the profound differences in the core features of multi-territory SVODs relative to linear ad-supported channels. Even though markets outside Europe don't have the same regulatory histories, many are reasonably uncertain about what foreign SVODs mean for their national video ecosystems; even if they aren't competitors, they are foreign, and they are exacerbating ecosystem adjustments begun by digital transmission, the establishment of digital channels, and the fragmentation that resulted. Netflix is also able to take advantage of local production incentives in many places, which brings down costs; however, it must be asked whether those incentives produce good value to the taxpayers supporting them.

Beyond these practical and corporate-relations strategies, multinational commissioning is consistent with Netflix's content aims. Good stories can come from anywhere. Netflix is incentivised to develop creative content just a bit outside of what can be done within the legacy system, and relying on a multi-territory distribution of creatives supports these aims. Netflix's recommendation and interface tools also make it possible to connect subscribers with content of interest, even if they wouldn't think to look for a series produced outside their own country.

Notably, there is often good alignment between Netflix and the non-advertiser-funded public-service broadcasters (PSBs) that have tended to produce content different from ad-supported services. Rather than perceiving that alignment as competition, especially in places in which PSBs face constant funding threats, it would be valuable to identify strategies for symbiotic benefit. Given that it seems unlikely that local commissions drive a considerable number of subscribers to Netflix, the type of co-commissioning deals evident between the ABC (AU) and Netflix appear somewhat symbiotic. With Netflix providing significant budget support, the ABC is able to stretch its programme budget and finance more and higher quality series. Both services get the kind of distinctive programming they seek, although whether content is place-based with cultural specificity (*The Mechanism*, *Girls from Ipanema*) or merely placed in country (as in *Money Heist* or *Lupin*) may reveal their different priorities. The trick to the symbiosis is in the distribution agreement. A reasonable, though rarely utilized, compromise is non-exclusive, multi-year rights for both partners. In other words, the ABC should have rights to broadcast in Australia and keep it available on its iView catch-up service in perpetuity (especially if public funds and supports are accessed in financing the series), while Netflix should have full-world access from debut, including in Australia. It really shouldn't matter whether Australians watch it on Netflix or the ABC, given that public-funded PSBs need not construct linear audiences in the same way as their ad-supported brethren (although this lazy metric is often used).

Netflix obviously has its reasons for multi-territory commissioning, and these probably derive from data about viewer behaviour that it keeps guarded. Examining what is available – the titles, the libraries, interviews with creatives and executives – offers hints. Although identifying a consistent Netflix content strategy for internationalization isn't possible, it is possible to consider how its local commissions deviate from and perpetuate the norms of those markets. In discussing the origin of South Korea's *Kingdom*, Netflix executive Minyoung Kim describes asking Eun-hee Kim about the show she'd dreamed of making but couldn't make given the norms and conventions of the South Korean industry.[14] It would be helpful to know how many other Netflix commissions offered similar opportunity in creatives' eyes.

As a multinational video service, Netflix must be explored as part of a longer history in which different mechanisms have internationalized video businesses. However, as an SVOD, it is unlikely to walk in lockstep with mechanisms such as foreign programme sales, co-production, format sales, and transnational satellite channels that have been the objects of investigation to date. And to bring all the arguments full circle, it is also likely that whatever might be said about it as a multinational SVOD applies largely only to Netflix rather than as characteristic of the SVOD sector. It remains fairly early days – especially in terms of multinational services. There is much yet to be developed and uncovered.

Part II Conclusion

Although SVODs generally are substantively distinguishable from the video distribution technologies that form many of our perceptions about how these industries should work, what they are likely to do, and the key debates that emerge in the field as a result, Netflix differs remarkably from other SVODs. It may be that greater uniformity among SVODs emerges in time, but the distinctions in their underlying characteristics also explain why there may be considerable variation over the long term. A key indication will be whether there comes to be greater consistency among their structuring characteristics. At this point, there just aren't enough cases of different configurations – nor have most services been available long enough – to make more definite assertions. But analysis of the various structuring characteristic combinations, and tying them to different strategies, offers tools that explain persistent discrepancies among services and shifts in library or content that result from their differences.

Conclusion

The role of SVODs in the video ecosystem is complicated, and more than a little misunderstanding surrounds them. A lot of that misunderstanding derives from assumptions of uniformity within the sector, which just isn't the case. Nor is it true that Netflix is representative of the sector. Misunderstanding also derives from both the hegemonies created by decades of linear ad-supported services dominating the sector and the thinking that comes from Hollywood box-office strategy. Even people in the industry who can see how lining up different characteristics in the slot-machine reels of SVOD leads to differentiation among services are so entrenched in decades of competitive norms and dynamics that they can miss the differences of the SVOD field. Given that most of these differences are entirely unclear to viewers sitting in front of sets, it is no wonder misperceptions persist.

Why is it important to appreciate the differences among SVODs and between SVODs and linear ad-supported services? Understanding these underlying economic dynamics helps explain actions taken by these companies that may not be highlighted in press releases and gives us hints about the future. These are particularly important matters for regulators and the actions that citizens, legislators, and industry imagine regulators taking. Just as it has taken more than a decade for governments to understand the many, varied, and multiple markets in which companies such as Facebook, Google, Amazon, and Apple compete – and how that dynamic requires much more precision than simply 'reining in big tech' – twenty-first-century audiovisual policy can only achieve its aims if it begins from appreciating the complexity of the ecosystem. In order to understand how market power may be operating, we must first recognize the different markets involved.

Policy-makers around the world are grappling with the challenge of reassessing appropriate policy for twenty-first-century audiovisual sectors, the limitations of old policy tools, and the new challenges introduced by digitization and building regulatory systems that account for the discrepant affordances and markets of different audiovisual technologies. For example, should domestically owned services face different local content obligations from those based outside the country? Should annual revenues govern policy application or be used as the basis of special corporate 'taxes' for foreign video providers? Should services with different value propositions be regulated in the same way? For example, in the current unregulated Australian SVOD market, domestic service Stan and Netflix provide different value propositions in relation to Australian content that make them more complementary than substitutable. But the government has proposed applying Australian content quotas to foreign global services.

Conclusion

Such a policy might negatively affect Stan by making Netflix more of a substitute. If this policy weakens the domestic provider's competitive position, would this policy ultimately advance or hinder Australians' access to Australian productions – the supposed goal of cultural policies?

The launch of Disney+ and AppleTV+ in late 2019 and the services that followed in 2020 made it clear that SVODs are no longer an emergent video technology but now the focus of industries built on decades of creating content for linear ad-supported services. Despite the many new services launching, we remain far from fully appreciating the dynamics of the 'post-network era' I've been trying to sort out for nearly two decades. As Netflix illustrated, major shifts such as a change in distribution technology and revenue model introduce many complications to past practices on industry operation further down the chain. The launch of owned-IP SVODs has only just started to change the flow of programmes that have long been sold and resold to national channels seeking to attract attention that can be sold to advertisers. Many of those ad-supported channels are under pressure from loss of income as advertisers move more dollars to search (Google, Amazon) and social media. The US has begun to show contraction in the linear channel market, and Disney has announced the closing of scores of channels around the globe. Although extensive downscaling is certain to come, this needn't be the 'death' of channels; rather, it could simply be an adjustment to the new market conditions. The best forecasts are rooted in the specific and nuanced segmentation of video sectors argued for here. Appreciating the complex dynamics will help explain how the failure of this or that service isn't a referendum on a sector but is derived from its particular characteristics or a strategy poorly aligned with its characteristics.

Much remains unknown, and prognostication is cheap and abundant. To be clear, this book explores SVODs in depth and detail because we lack a strong conceptual basis for such services – not because they are dominant now or likely to be so anytime soon. Their novelty unquestionably leads to a disproportionate amount of cultural attention and pontification, even though linear services remain dominant in terms of viewing time and access. SVODs are a significant and growing part of the audiovisual ecosystem of many countries, and the industrial distinctions highlighted here are important to establish because they position the services to play distinctive cultural functions in comparison with previous distribution technologies. There are many questions to investigate and cultural conceptualizations to be built with these industrial distinctions in mind.

I have more questions than answers about the next decade. I'm mostly curious to see how closely any of the owned-IP SVODs come to reproducing Netflix's particular global strategy and how many of them find a way to persist if they don't. I'm also curious about the content strategies that emerge from the owned-IP companies and whether their bespoke SVOD content comes to be more distinctive. And I'm curious to see the role of territory-specific and content-specific services. They have received short shrift here and been steadily undervalued in this first phase of SVOD services. Market analysis suggests there is a fair bit of opportunity for services offering a value proposition different from that of global general SVODs. There is room for a lot of different winners here. Many won't be

Conclusion

household names recognized globally, but that doesn't diminish how profoundly they might adjust the availability of stories for viewers in particular locations or with particular tastes.

It is too soon, in 2022, to make strong declarations about SVODs as a category or to be clear about their role in the broader ecosystem. This book offers a starting point for tracking adjustment as the norms of these services and their relation to those that have been in the marketplace continue to evolve.

Notes

Introduction

1 The video on demand offered by US cable services are somewhat confusing to classify. Because they are offered by 'cable' companies, they might seem distinct from internet-distributed video, but they do use the same technology. Their underlying business foundations differ from those commonly considered SVODs – such as Netflix or Disney+; cable providers have offered on-demand access as part of paying for large bundles of linear channels (such as Xfinity from Comcast), so they differ in this regard. For the purposes of this book, on demand requires internet distribution. See Johnson, *Online TV*, for an account that takes on analysis of the broader category of internet-distributed video.

2 Some of these services are confusingly called BVOD (broadcast video on demand) – confusing because BVOD is not a parallel category to AVOD or SVOD such that the B would denote a different type of funding. Instead, B signals a service operated by a company that also operates a broadcast channel, and notably these might

rely on advertising or public funding. Many began as catch-up services but increasingly license content that is not part of linear schedules.

3 Generally, so long as commercial video services don't require payment to access, they are best understood as AVOD and not part of the phenomenon explored here. The British context is particularly tricky, with many commercial channels that also have significant public-service expectations that have distinguished them from what are described here as commercial, linear, ad-supported services. The logics of these services in terms of strategy may not perfectly align with those that are purely commercially oriented. Similarly, a service such as Britbox may not perfectly adhere to the 'rules' here but operates largely as a SVOD comparable to those discussed here.

4 The ideas here are a refinement of thinking initially developed with Ramon Lobato in Lobato and Lotz, 'Beyond streaming wars'.

5 See Lobato, *Netflix Nations*, p. 69.

6 Data in table 1 drawn from Ampere Analysis. Data based on February 2021, except for Crunchyroll (October 2020) and Paramount+ (March 2021). Libraries based on US library, except for Stan, which is based on the Australian library.

7 In some cases, it may be difficult to discern the distinction. For example, Disney+ is a corporate extension, though the video business could also be argued as a corporate complement. The finer details can be considered in specific cases as they matter; I'd suggest the percentage of corporate revenue is a good piece of data for sorting the central business(es) of a conglomerate.

8 For more detailed exploration of the implications of bundling, see Lotz, *Portals*.

9 See Spigel, 'Introduction'. Catherine Johnson also suggests some useful distinctions in her consideration

of the broader category of internet-distributed video in *Online TV*.
10 A more sophisticated dichotomy is of durable and ephemeral video, as discussed in Lotz, *Media Disrupted*.
11 Based on data collected by DP190100978.
12 Rather, for Netflix, theatrical distribution is used to achieve eligibility for awards and to attract creative talent that prioritizes theatrical release.
13 See Netflix Film Project at https://netflixoriginalmovies reviewed.wordpress.com/2018/03/28/about-this-blog/.
14 Technically, linear, subscriber-funded services such as HBO used this strategy first, though such services were fairly uncommon.

Chapter 1   Experience

1 Lotz, 'Binging isn't quite the word'.
2 Klein, 'Why you watch what you watch when you watch'.
3 https://futureofstorytelling.org/speaker/todd-yellin.
4 Rubin, 'Television uses and gratifications'.

Chapter 2   Building Libraries

1 A deeper discussion of the bundled SVOD through the lens of private subscription libraries of the eighteenth century can be found in Lotz, *Portals*.
2 See Johnson, *Branding Television*.

Chapter 3   Subscriber Funding

1 Advertisers and ad-supported services have negotiated the value of this later viewing – and the likelihood of commercial skipping in different ways – and, in some

cases, services are able to sell some of this attention. But
the goal is live attention.

2 Lotz, 'Channel bundles persist'.
3 Smith and Telang, *Streaming, Sharing, Stealing.*
4 Owen and Wildman, *Video Economics.*
5 Notably, this practice was mostly characteristic of US
production; other countries did not tie 'success' to such
long runs and had norms of shorter seasons/series.
6 Adalian, 'Inside the binge factory'.

Chapter 4   Licensing, Labour, Regulation, and Recommendation

1 How this works inside an owned-IP SVOD is unclear.
2 Caves, *Creative Industries.*
3 SVODs do require internet infrastructure, but this is
not bespoke to video services in the manner of cable
and satellite. Countries built internet infrastructure for
reasons quite separate from video service.
4 Hesmondhalgh and Lotz, 'Video screen interfaces as
new sites of media circulation power'.
5 See discussion in Lotz, *Portals.*

Chapter 5   Scale and Specialization

1 Due to changes in Netflix's reporting of subscribers, the
horizon of this data is not very long; however, to see
the trendline of commissioning back to 2015, consider
figure 5.
2 Analysis of Ampere Data, March 2021; see also figure 2.
3 Nine Entertainment Annual Report 2020; conversion to
US$ × 1.3 = AU$.
4 Todd Spangler, 'Crunchyroll inks deal with Idris and
Sabrina Elba for dark fantasy anime series', *Variety,* 2

February 2021; https://variety.com/2021/digital/news/
idris-elba-sabirna-elba-crunchyroll-anime-1234898245/.

5 'WWE Network hits record 2.1 million subscribers', 9
April 2018; https://corporate.wwe.com/investors/news/
press-releases/2018/04-09-2018-204506063.

6 Hulu tried a launch in Japan in 2011 but gave up in
2014; it sold the service to Nippon TV and licensed the
label so that it is Hulu in name only.

7 Sharon Masige, 'Stan is beefing up its original content to
more than 30 productions a year for the next five years',
Business Insider, 24 August 2020; www.businessinsider.
com.au/stan-expands-original-content-2020-8.

8 See *Variety*/Ampere analysis of France (https://variety.
com/2020/tv/news/france-osc-svod-orange-
1234720166/); Germany (https://variety.com/2020/tv/
news/joyn-germany-prosiebensat-1-discovery-
1234720206/); the Middle East (https://variety.com/
2020/streaming/global/mbc-group-shahid-netflix-
middle-east-1234720035/); and India (https://variety.
com/2020/streaming/global/india-streamer-altbalaji-
1234720333/).

9 Doyle and Paterson, 'Public policy and independent
television production in the UK'.

Chapter 6   The Discrepant Field of Global Services

1 The ideas in this chapter were worked through with
Ramon Lobato in a co-authored article published in
Media Industries, Lobato and Lotz, 'Beyond streaming
wars'; we also talk about them in this article, originally
published in *The Conversation* for a more general
audience than I assume here. Amanda Lotz and Ramon
Lobato, 'Why the streaming wars are a myth', *Fast
Company*, 9 November 2019; https://www.fastcompany.
com/90428525/why-the-streaming-wars-are-a-myth

2 Lotz, Potter, and Johnson, 'Understanding the changing television market'.
3 Lotz, 'In between the global and the local'.
4 Though the different norms of the US versus those of much of the rest of the world have added layers of confusion. Catch-up services have played a comparatively minor role in the US. This is explained by the role cable VOD played there. Also Hulu functioned as a catch-up service but has always also had SVOD features, further complicating comparison. In contrast, catch-up services were often earlier to market outside the US and provided viewers' first experience (norm) of on-demand viewing. Netflix introduced viewers to an experience difficult for catch-up services to emulate because they are quite different in business terms.

Part I Conclusion

1 'Web series' also does not work as a term for content created for internet-distributed services because the industrial dynamics of those services have considerable internal variation.

Chapter 7   Netflix Content Concepts and Vocabulary

1 Adalian, 'Inside the binge factory'.
2 Barrett, 'Netflix's grand, daring, maybe crazy plan to conquer the world'.
3 Rodriguez, 'Netflix divides its 93 million users around the world into 1,300 "taste communities"'.
4 Madrigal, 'How Netflix reverse-engineered Hollywood'.
5 Cinema loyalty clubs enable some information, but notably this resides with exhibitors, not studios. Video rental stores also could have developed this type of

perspective but lacked a mechanism to use it to guide content creation.

Chapter 8 Netflix Library Strategies

1 Analysis of data accessed through subscription to Ampere Analysis SVOD Analytics data, January 2021.
2 Lotz, 'In between the global and the local'.
3 For analysis of early commissioning strategy, see Lotz, 'What's going on?'.
4 Amanda D. Lotz, Oliver Eklund, and Stuart Soroka, 'Netflix, library analysis and globalization: rethinking flow as circulation'. In development.
5 This dynamic is somewhat simpler for Netflix because all of its commissions are bespoke to the service. In contrast, owned-IP SVODs have many titles that they own but that were not developed specifically for the service. Although I apply this analysis only to Netflix, I would argue that owned IP should be considered as licensed content in performing similar analysis of other SVODs.
6 Netflix failed to secure global rights for its first series, but the general strategy is universal availability.
7 The precise percentage varies by national library, with more variation among Amazon Prime Video libraries. The figures offered are generally representative.
8 Analysis of data accessed through subscription to Ampere Analysis SVOD Analytics data, January 2021.
9 This proved to be a significant issue in preventing the development of substantially niche cable channels. See Lotz, *We Now Disrupt This Broadcast*.
10 Several SVODs have launched from companies operating linear channels. This analysis does not consider commissioned series available on both the linear and the SVOD as SVOD originals. The Ampere data does not allow

us to separate the few titles created, for example, for Disney+ from those generally created by Disney, so this figure excludes the owned-IP services.

11 Owen and Wildman, *Video Economics*.

Chapter 9 Netflix Content Strategies

1 See Lotz, *We Now Disrupt This Broadcast*.
2 Mittell, *Complex TV*.
3 Kay, 'Local language content top most popular Netflix releases of 2019 in eight countries'.
4 Adalian, 'Inside the binge factory'.

Chapter 10 Netflix's Approach to Being Global

1 Chalaby, *Transnational Television Worldwide*; Cunningham and Jacka, *Australian Television and International Mediascapes*; Flew, Iosifidis, and Steemers, *Global Media and National Policies*; Sinclair, Jacka, and Cunningham, *New Patterns in Global Television*; Steemers, *Selling Television*; Straubhaar, *World Television*.
2 Limov, 'Click it, binge it, get hooked'.
3 More detailed account in Amanda D. Lotz, Oliver Eklund, and Stuart Soroka, 'Netflix, library analysis and globalization: rethinking flow as circulation'. In development.
4 Lotz, 'In between the global and the local'.
5 Lobato and Scarlata, 'Australian content in SVOD catalogs'.
6 Netflix Fourth Quarter 2020 Earnings Interview, 19 January 2021; https://ir.netflix.net/investor-news-and-events/investor-events/event-details/2021/Netflix-Fourth-Quarter-2020-Earnings-Interview/default.

aspx; 'The Gauge Shows Streaming is Taking a Seat at the Table', 17 June 2021; www.nielsen.com/us/en/insights/article/2021/the-gauge-shows-streaming-takes-a-seat-at-the-table/.

7 Straubhaar and La Pastina, 'Multiple proximities between television genres and audiences'.

8 Reed Hastings, DealBook Conference, 6 November 2019; www.youtube.com/watch?v=7V6FFeZdFz4.

9 Malte Ketelsen, Marlene Stocker, Michael Ball and Samuel Stolton, 'Storytelling and multilingualism at Netflix', *EURACTIV*, 16 January 2020; www.euractiv.com/section/digital/video/storytelling-and-multilingualism-at-netflix/.

10 Presentation by Sofia Mavros, Senior Researcher, Consumer Insights, Asia Pacific, Netflix, Screen Forever, 16 February 2021.

11 'The 2019 Drama Summit Sessions: Kelly Luegenbiehl', 19 December 2019; www.c21media.net/c21podcasts/the-2019-drama-summit-sessions-kelly-luegenbiehl/.

12 Notably, the series was not originally developed as set in Australia and was first pitched in the US, so the 'Australianness' was added later. *Tidelands* thus might not be a good case of Netflix trying to go all in on local specificity.

13 Cunningham and Scarlata, 'New forms of internationalisation?'.

14 Patrick Frater, '*Kingdom* screenwriter Kim Eun-hee celebrates expanding opportunities', *Variety*, 8 March 2021; https://variety.com/2021/artisans/asia/kingdom-screenwriter-kim-eun-hee-womens-impact-1234924622/?.

References

Adalian, Josef, 'Inside the binge factory', *New York Magazine*, 11 June 2018; www.vulture.com/2018/06/how-netflix-swallowed-tv-industry.html.

Barrett, Brian, 'Netflix's grand, daring, maybe crazy plan to conquer the world', *Wired*, 27 March 2016; www.wired.com/2016/03/netflixs-grand-maybe-crazy-plan-conquer-world/.

Caves, Richard E., *Creative Industries: Contracts between Art and Commerce*. Cambridge, MA: Harvard University Press, 2000.

Chalaby, Jean K., ed., *Transnational Television Worldwide: Towards a New Media Order*. London: Tauris, 2005.

Cunningham, Stuart, and Elizabeth Jacka, *Australian Television and International Mediascapes*. Cambridge: Cambridge University Press, 1996.

Cunningham, Stuart, and Alexa Scarlata, 'New forms of internationalisation? The impact of Netflix in Australia', *Media International Australia* 177/1 (2020): 149–64; https://journals.sagepub.com/doi/full/10.1177/1329878X20941173.

Doyle, Gillian, and Richard Paterson, 'Public policy and independent television production in the UK', *Journal of Media Business Studies* 5/3 (2008): 17–33; www.tandfonline.com/doi/abs/10.1080/16522354.2008.1107 3473.

Flew, Terry, Petros Iosifidis, and Jeanette Steemers, *Global Media and National Policies: The Return of the State*. Basingstoke: Palgrave, 2017.

Hesmondhalgh, David, and Lotz, Amanda D., 'Video screen interfaces as new sites of media circulation power', *International Journal of Communication* 14 (2020): 1–24; https://ijoc.org/index.php/ijoc/article/view/13261.

Jenkins, Henry, *Convergence Culture: Where Old and New Media Collide*. New York: New York University Press, 2006.

Johnson, Catherine, *Branding Television*. Abingdon: Routledge, 2012.

Johnson, Catherine, *Online TV*. Abingdon: Routledge, 2019.

Kay, Jeremy, 'Local language content top most popular Netflix releases of 2019 in eight countries', *ScreenDaily*, 31 December 2019; www.screendaily.com/news/local-language-content-top-most-popular-netflix-releases-of-2019-in-eight-countries/5145879.article.

Klein, Paul, 'Why you watch what you watch when you watch', in J. S. Harris, ed., *TV Guide: The First 25 Years*. New York: New American Library, 1978, pp. 186–8 [orig. pubd in TV *Guide*, July 1971].

Limov, Brad, 'Click it, binge it, get hooked: Netflix and the growing US audience for foreign content', *International Journal of Communication* 14 (2020): 6304–23; https://ijoc.org/index.php/ijoc/article/view/16343/3301.

Lobato, Ramon, *Netflix Nations: The Geography of Digital Distribution*. New York: New York University Press, 2019.

Lobato, Ramon, and Amanda D. Lotz, 'Beyond streaming

References

wars: rethinking competition in video services', *Media Industries* 8/1 (2021); https://doi.org/10.3998/mij.1338.

Lobato, Ramon, and Alexa Scarlata, *Australian Content in SVOD Catalogs: Availability and Discoverability – 2019 Edition*. Melbourne: RMIT University, 2019; https://apo.org.au/node/264821.

Lotz, Amanda D., 'Binging isn't quite the word', *Antenna*, 29 October 2014; http://blog.commarts.wisc.edu/2014/10/29/binging-isnt-quite-the-word/.

Lotz, Amanda D., 'Channel bundles persist – for now – despite digital disruption', Media Industries Project/Carsey-Wolf Center, January 2015; www.carseywolf.ucsb.edu/wp-content/uploads/2018/02/Lotz_ChannelBundles.pdf.

Lotz, Amanda D., *Portals: A Treatise on Internet-Distributed Television*. Ann Arbor, MI: Maize Books, 2017.

Lotz, Amanda D., *We Now Disrupt This Broadcast: How Cable Transformed Television and the Internet Revolutionized it All*. Cambridge, MA: MIT Press, 2018.

Lotz, Amanda D., 'In between the global and the local: mapping the geographies of Netflix as a multinational service', *International Journal of Cultural Studies* 24/2 (2021): 195–215.

Lotz, Amanda D., *Media Disrupted: Surviving Pirates, Cannibals, and Streaming Wars*. Cambridge, MA: MIT Press, 2021.

Lotz, Amanda D., 'What's going on? Netflix and the commissioning of *Sense8*', in Deborah Shaw and Rob Stone, eds, *Sense8: Transcending Television*. London: Bloomsbury, 2021, pp. 31–40.

Lotz, Amanda D., Anna Potter, and Catherine Johnson, 'Understanding the changing television market: a comparison of the macroeconomy of the

References

United States, the United Kingdom, and Australia',
*Convergence: The International Journal of Research
into New Media Technologies* (2021); https://doi.
org/10.1177/13548565211028205.

Madrigal, Alexis C., 'How Netflix reverse-engineered
Hollywood', *The Atlantic*, 3 January 2015; www.
theatlantic.com/technology/archive/2014/01/
how-netflix-reverse-engineered-hollywood/282679/.

Mittell, Jason, *Complex TV: The Poetics of Contemporary
Television Storytelling*. New York: New York University
Press, 2015.

Owen, Bruce M., and Steven Wildman, *Video Economics*.
Cambridge, MA: Harvard University Press, 1992.

Rodriguez, Ashley, 'Netflix divides its 93 million users
around the world into 1,300 "taste communities"',
Quartz, 22 March 2017; https://qz.com/939195/netflix-
nflx-divides-its-93-million-users-around-the-world-not-
by-geography-but-into-1300-taste-communities/.

Rubin, Alan M., 'Television uses and gratifications: the
interactions of viewing patterns and motivations',
Journal of Broadcasting & Electronic Media 27/1
(1983): 37–51.

Sinclair, John, Elizabeth Jacka, and Stuart Cunningham,
New Patterns in Global Television: Peripheral Vision.
Oxford: Oxford University Press, 1996.

Smith, Michael D., and Rahul Telang, *Streaming, Sharing,
Stealing: Big Data and the Future of Entertainment*.
Cambridge, MA: MIT Press, 2016.

Spigel, Lynn, 'Introduction', in Lynn Spigel and Jan
Olsson, eds, *Television after TV: Essays on a Medium in
Transition*. Durham, NC: Duke University Press, 2004,
pp. 1–40.

Steemers, Jeanette, *Selling Television: British Television in
the Global Marketplace*. London: British Film Institute,
2004.

References

Straubhaar, Joseph D., *World Television: From Global to Local*. Thousand Oaks, CA: Sage, 2007.

Straubhaar, Joseph D., and Antonio C. La Pastina, 'Multiple proximities between television genres and audiences', in Straubhaar, *World Television: From Global to Local*. Thousand Oaks, CA: Sage, 2007, pp. 195–220.

Williams, Raymond, *Television: Technology and Cultural Form*. 2nd edn, London: Routledge, 1990.

Index

Index

Index

Index

Index